Grammar, Punctuation and Spelling

Revision and Practice

Louise Moore

Rising Stars UK Ltd, 7 Hatchers Mews, Bermondsey Street, London SE1 3GS
www.risingstars-uk-com

Every effort has been made to trace copyright holders and obtain their permission for the use of copyright material. The authors and publishers will gladly receive information enabling them to rectify any error or omission in subsequent editions.

All facts are correct at time of going to press.

© 2012
Published 2012
Reprinted 2012 (twice), 2013

Text, design and layout © Rising Stars UK Ltd
Cover design: Burville-Riley Design
Design: David Blundell, Branford Graphics
Layout: Words & Pictures Ltd, London
Editorial: Dawn Booth
Proofreader: Margaret Crowther
Illustrations: Phill Burrows (Teachers and Students), p. 56 (top right) iStock / Mike Elliott, p. 56 (top centre) iStock / Kemie, p. 56 (top left) iStock / Ibrahim Sari, p. 56 bottom right iStock / dedMazay, p. 56 (bottom left) iStock / Brett Lamb, all others Emily Skinner

British Library Cataloguing in Publication Data
A CIP record for this book is available from the British Library.

ISBN: 978-0-85769-616-8

Printed by Craftprint International, Singapore

Contents

Answers are in the centre of the book and can be pulled out before handing to the child.

How to use this book

(**1**) Important facts and skills are given at the top of each section. Read them carefully – they show what you really need to know.

(**2**) There is an example question for you to read through. Follow the steps carefully, then try to work through the example yourself.

(**3**) Top tips are given on many pages – they are hints to help you do your best and make learning easier and more fun. Use them well!

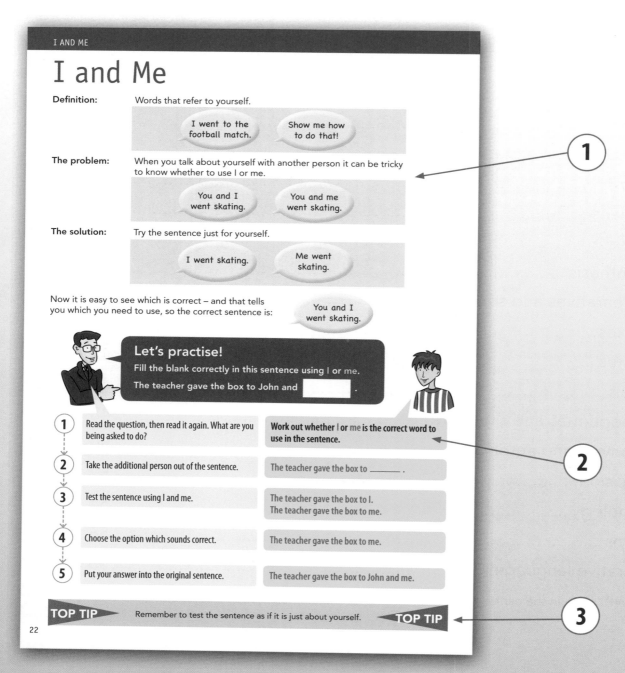

4 Each section has a set of practice questions. Each question has a space for you to write in the answer and a specific number of marks (as in a real National Test). Answers are included in the middle, although your teacher may remove these pages! Marking guidance is provided.

5 Questions are asked in lots of different ways to check that you really understand the topic.

6 If you feel confident with the topic, each section finishes with a challenge. This is a chance to push yourself a little bit further and see what you can achieve!

7 You will see the assessment panel at the top of each set of practice questions. Colour in the face that best describes your understanding of the topic and how you did. Use the spelling tests in the centre of the book to help you learn and practise your spelling.

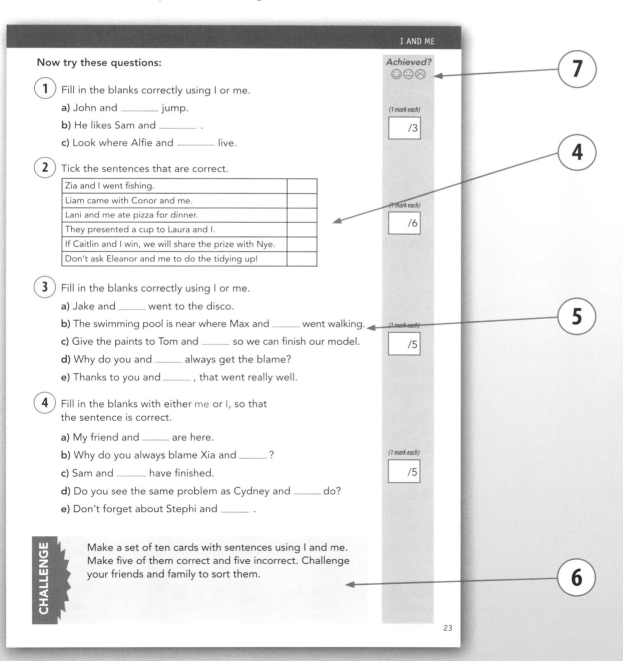

I AND ME

Now try these questions:

Achieved?
☺ 😐 ☹   **7**

1 Fill in the blanks correctly using I or me.

a) John and _____ jump.

b) He likes Sam and _____ .

c) Look where Alfie and _____ live.

(1 mark each)

/3

4

2 Tick the sentences that are correct.

Zia and I went fishing.	
Liam came with Conor and me.	
Lani and me ate pizza for dinner.	
They presented a cup to Laura and I.	
If Caitlin and I win, we will share the prize with Nye.	
Don't ask Eleanor and me to do the tidying up!	

(1 mark each)

/6

3 Fill in the blanks correctly using I or me.

a) Jake and _____ went to the disco.

b) The swimming pool is near where Max and _____ went walking.

c) Give the paints to Tom and _____ so we can finish our model.

d) Why do you and _____ always get the blame?

e) Thanks to you and _____ , that went really well.

5

(1 mark each)

/5

4 Fill in the blanks with either me or I, so that the sentence is correct.

a) My friend and _____ are here.

b) Why do you always blame Xia and _____ ?

c) Sam and _____ have finished.

d) Do you see the same problem as Cydney and _____ do?

e) Don't forget about Stephi and _____ .

(1 mark each)

/5

CHALLENGE

Make a set of ten cards with sentences using I and me. Make five of them correct and five incorrect. Challenge your friends and family to sort them.

6

23

5

Revision of word classes

These are the word classes that you should already be familiar with.

Word class	Explanation
Articles	the words a, an or the that come before a noun
Nouns	names of a person, animal, place, thing or idea
Pronouns	take the place of a noun in a sentence
Adjectives	describe nouns
Verbs	give an action or happening
Adverbs	give more information about verbs
Conjunctions	connectives used to link different ideas in a sentence
Connectives	link different phrases, sentences and paragraphs together
Prepositions	show the position of things

Let's practise!
Which word classes does the word **light** belong to?

1 Read the question, then read it again. What are you being asked to do?

Work out the word classes that the word **light** could belong to.

2 Work out the classes that definitely don't contain **light**.

It can't be an article, a pronoun, a conjunction or connective.

3 Could it be a noun?

Yes – a light is the name of an object.

4 Could it be an adjective?

Yes – something could be light to carry.

5 Could it be a verb?

Yes – you can light a fire.

6 Could it be an adverb?

No – you could run lightly, not light.

7 Could it be a preposition?

No – light can't relate two things.

8 Write your answer.

Light can be a noun, an adjective or a verb.

TOP TIP
It is sometimes thought to be poor grammar to end a sentence with a preposition. This won't always be possible, but try to avoid ending sentences with words such as:
at   by   for   on   to   up   upon   with
TOP TIP

Now try these questions:

1 Which word classes can these words belong to?

a) date _____

(2 marks)

b) hard _____

(2 marks)

c) rush _____

(3 marks)

d) prime _____

(3 marks)

e) coat _____

(2 marks)

/12

2 Write the correct label in each box:
ART for Article   N for Noun   V for Verb   ADV for Adverb
ADJ for Adjective   C for Connective   P for Preposition

Suddenly,	we	saw	a	shape	emerge	from	the	shadows.

The	dogs	howled	because	of	the	fireworks.

Eat	healthy	foods	while	you	are	growing.

Although	it	is	cold,	I	am	going.

(1 mark for every 2 correct)

/15

3 Build sentences using the types of words shown in the boxes.

connective	article	adjective	noun

verb	adverb

noun	verb	adverb	preposition

article	noun	adjective	noun

article	adjective	noun	verb

connective	pronoun	adverb	verb

(1 mark for every 2 correct)

/11

CHALLENGE

List all the types of each word class that you know and then try to find some more.

Nouns

There are different types of nouns. Have a look at the table and see which of them you recognise.

Type of noun	Explanation	Examples
abstract	name of something that can't be felt or touched	anger, love, honesty, thoughtfulness
collective	name for a group of things	flock, herd, pack, library, swarm
common	name for an ordinary object or animal	cat, table, cup
proper	the name of a particular person, place or thing	Paris, Fred, Brazil, Spanish
uncountable	something that can't be counted, often used with words such as much or a little bit	water, air, life, milk, music

Let's practise!

Match each noun to the correct label.

jealousy	team	French	travel
uncountable noun	abstract noun	collective noun	proper noun

1 Read the question, then read it again. What are you being asked to do?

Decide on the type of noun.

2 Check for the most straightforward noun.

We need a proper noun. It will be the name of something and start with a capital letter. It must be French.

3 Check for the next most straightforward noun.

We need a collective noun. It will be a word that is used for a group of something. It must be team.

4 Check for the next most straightforward noun.

We need an abstract noun. It will be a word that is used for a feeling or quality. It must be jealousy.

5 Check the remaining answer.

Travel – this is a noun that we can't count, so it is an uncountable noun.

jealousy	team	French	travel
uncountable noun	abstract noun	collective noun	proper noun

Now try these questions:

1 Write the nouns in the correct boxes. Some words will go in more than one box.

bravery London weather Harry clarinet happiness family art health chair New York advice English curiosity bag Uncle Gary company freedom trust bus army furniture fear electricity

Abstract nouns	Collective nouns	Common nouns	Proper nouns	Uncountable nouns

(1 mark each each correct entry)

/33

2 Circle all the nouns in these sentences.
a) When Charlotte's anger affected her work, she had to eat chocolate.
b) When a bunch of flowers arrived, Miss Lomas's embarrassment showed.
c) Harvey got the help he needed with his homework from Rio.
d) The greed of some children is a problem for everyone.
e) The school council had an agreement with Mrs Hartley about playground equipment.

(1 mark for each sentence)

/5

3 Write the collective nouns for these groups, using your dictionary to help you.
a) _____ of beauties   b) _____ of elephants
c) _____ of ants   d) _____ of geese
e) _____ of kittens   f) _____ of lions
g) _____ of beavers   h) _____ of owls
i) _____ of crows   j) _____ of whales

(1 mark each)

/10

4 Write a capital letter at the start of each proper noun in these sentences.
a) My first school was called gleadless primary school.
b) The best book about cats is called the cat kingdom.
c) My favourite uncle is uncle tom.
d) At headless cross there is thought to be a headless ghost.
e) Whaley memorial park is a fantastic park to visit.

(1 mark for each line)

/5

 **CHALLENGE** Find all the uncountable nouns you can. Can you think of a way to group the nouns you found?

Subject, object and verb

To understand sentences, it is helpful to be able to identify the basic units (main parts). These are the subject, object and verb (sometimes called the predicate).

	Informal	Formal
subject	the person or thing doing the action	agrees with the verb
object	the person or thing affected by or receiving the action	does not affect the verb
verb	the action being done	known as the predicate

To check if a noun is the subject or object use this simple test:

1 Change the verb to the simple present tense (or a continuous form using –ing, e.g. working).
2 Change the noun from singular to plural and check if you need to change the verb.
3 If the answer is yes, then the noun you changed is the subject.
  If the answer is no, then the noun you changed is the object.

Let's practise!
Find the subject, object and verb in this sentence.

> **The children in the class determined the arrangement of the tables.**

1 Read the question, then read it again. What are you being asked to do?

Find the subject, verb and object (also known as the predicate).

2 What is the verb?

The thing being done is determined.

3 Is the subject easy to identify?

No. It could be children or tables.

4 Check the form of the verb.

It is in the past tense, so change it to the present: I determine, he determines, they determine. The children in the class determine the arrangement of the tables.
the table: The children in the class determine the arrangement of the table. This doesn't affect the verb.
the child: The child in the class determines the arrangement of the tables. This affects the verb so children is the subject.

5 Test the subject by changing the nouns to singulars and checking if they change the verb.

subject – the children   verb – determined
object – the tables

Now try these questions:

1 Underline the subject and highlight the verb (predicate) in these sentences.

a) The owl hoots.

b) A lady screamed.

c) The children were skipping.

d) The bus stopped.

e) They are busy.

f) The fire-engine is red.

(1 mark for each line)

/6

2 Complete the table.

Sentence	Subject	Object	Verb
The man washed the car.			
The trees were uprooted by the wind.			
Over the sea, the ship was sailing.			
The traffic jam went through Manchester.			
Across the lawn danced the fairies.			

(1 mark for each cell)

/15

3 Identify the word in bold as the subject or object of the sentence.

a) Caitlin hammered the **pegs** into the ground. _____

b) Before bedtime, **Joshua** had read his magazine. _____

c) Running quickly, Lucy just managed to catch the **train**. _____

d) When it is sunny, **he** walks home. _____

e) The **stone**, which had been thrown by Eleanor, was very heavy. _____

(1 mark each)

/5

4 Decide whether the subject or the verb is missing and then complete the sentence with a suitable word.

a) _____ opened the door.

The subject / verb is missing.

b) John, was totally unreliable, _____ the cub meeting.

The subject / verb is missing.

c) Even though it was Sunday, _____ were too busy to sit and read.

The subject / verb is missing.

(2 marks for each line)

/6

 **CHALLENGE** Find out about compound subjects and verbs, explain what they are and write some sentences using them.

11

Active and passive sentences

Definitions: A sentence is **active** when the subject is doing the action (verb). For example:

The police car was following the lorry.

The **subject** is the police car. The **verb** is following. The **object** is the lorry. The police car is doing the following.

A sentence is **passive** when the subject has the action done to it. For example:

The lorry was being followed by the police car.

The **subject** is the lorry. The **verb** is followed. The **object** is the police car. The lorry is being followed.

Let's practise!
Change this sentence from the active to the passive voice.

> **George opened the door.**

1	Read the question, then read it again. What are you being asked to do?	**Change the sentence from the active to the passive voice.**
2	Work out what is the subject, the object and the verb.	**The subject is George. The object is the door. The verb is opened.**
3	Move the object to the position of the subject.	the door ...
4	Move the subject to the position of the object and write by before it.	the door ... **by** George.
5	Use the verb to be and change the verb to fit the new sentence.	**It's the past tense so to be will be was or were. The door is singular so you need was.**
6	Write the full sentence.	**The door was opened by George.**

> **TOP TIP**
>
> Sentences in the active voice are easier to read and understand, so it is generally better to use the active voice.
> Use the passive voice:
> • when the person doing the action is unknown
> • if you don't want to say who did the action
> • for variety.
>
> **TOP TIP**

Now try these questions:

1 Join each sentence to the correct label.

Andy was interested in sport.		The class was taught by Mrs Butcher.
	active sentence	
The bus was hit by a car.		Caitlin won the race.
	passive sentence	
The man was arrested by the police.		Vikki was tested by Mrs Sellars.

(1 mark each)

/6

2 Write **A** after the sentences that are active and **P** after the sentences that are passive.
  a) The sheep was chased by the dog.
  b) A shoal of fish swam underneath the boat.
  c) The table was bought by Mrs Pattison.
  d) The students protested about the lack of aid to Africa.

(1 mark each)

/4

3 Change these passive sentences to active sentences.
  a) The cake had been eaten by the children.

  _____

  b) The game was being spoiled by the infants.

  _____

  c) The play was appreciated by the audience.

  _____

  d) The plants are hidden by the snow.

  _____

(1 mark for each line)

/4

4 Change these active sentences to passive sentences.
  a) James is chasing after Harvey.

  _____

  b) Megan is laughing at Skye.

  _____

  c) Mrs Mellor is helping Ms Wright.

  _____

(1 mark for each line)

/3

CHALLENGE

  1 Count all the passive sentences you can find in two pages of a book. Why do you think there are that many?

  2 Find some passive sentences in a reading book and change them to active sentences.

13

Phrases and clauses

Understanding phrases and clauses helps you to understand punctuation. Punctuation marks, such as commas, semi-colons and colons, are often required with either a phrase or a clause.

Definitions: A **phrase** is a group of words that may have nouns and verbs but does not have a subject doing a verb. For example:

> some frightening people   running down the hill
> going to the shops   after the terrible meal

A **clause** is a group of words that has a subject doing a verb. For example:

> he can lift a car   because she liked picking flowers
> when it is time to go home   Jake plays football

An **independent clause** can be a complete sentence by itself. For example:

> He can lift a car.   Jake plays football.

A **subordinate** (or **dependent**) **clause** starts with a subordinating conjunction and that means it doesn't make sense by itself. For example:

> when it is time to go home   because she liked picking flowers

Let's practise!

Circle any clauses and underline any phrases in this sentence.

> **Renowned for his sporting prowess, Barti raced to victory at the Winter Olympics.**

1	Read the question, then read it again. What are you being asked to do?	**Circle the clauses and underline the phrases.**
2	Split the sentence into sections.	**a) Renowned for his sporting prowess, b) Barti raced to victory c) at the Winter Olympics.**
3	Check if a subject is doing a verb in each section.	**a) no; b) yes; c) no**
4	If the answer is no, that must be a phrase.	**Renowned for his sporting prowess and at the Winter Olympics are phrases.**
5	If the answer is yes, that must be a clause.	**Barti raced to victory is a clause.**
6	Write the answer.	<u>Renowned for his sporting prowess,</u> (Barti raced to victory) <u>at the Winter Olympics.</u>

Now try these questions:

1 Write a **P** after a phrase and a **C** after a clause.

a) the dog barked
b) when they went skating
c) after a long time
d) because it was time
e) the blazing hot sun
f) many people saw the show
g) it rained all day
h) when he saw the parcel

(1 mark each)

/8

2 Circle the independent clauses and underline the dependent clause.

a) The dog whined when it heard the fireworks.
b) Because it was snowing, we built a large snowman.
c) We were allowed cake since it was my birthday.
d) Reece fell down so we had to abandon the race.
e) When Louie was away, we did a maths test.

(1 mark for each line)

/5

3 Match the groups of words to the correct label.

a large shaggy dog	phrase	clouds form over hills
despite the rain	independent clause	eating his dinner
as he lifted the lid		during the interval
the children were glad	dependent clause	when I go home

(1 mark each)

/8

4 In these sentences, highlight the phrases, underline the independent clauses and circle the dependent clauses.

a) Whilst watching the match, Sonal started to feel ill.
b) The forest was dark and gloomy; the mountains were light and airy.
c) The phone rang just as tea was ready.
d) When he saw the bill, Sam was very cross.

(1 mark for each line)

/4

5 Write an independent clause to complete these sentences.

a) While it was raining, _____ .
b) _____ after she finished her homework.
c) _____ because it was hot.

(1 mark for each line)

/3

CHALLENGE Take a passage from a book and list all the phrases, dependent clauses and independent clauses.
Which list is longest? Why do you think that is?

Adverbs and adverbials

Definitions: An **adverb** is a type of word (a single word) that describes a verb.

An **adverbial** is part of a sentence that tells us more about the verb (and can be more than one word). An adverb can be an adverbial. For example:

William will finish soon. Soon is an adverb that tells us when William will finish.

William will finish in a few minutes. In a few minutes is an adverbial that tells us when William will finish.

Both sentences give us similar information. Adverbials answer questions like:

	Examples
Where?	Tom hid the box under the stairs.
When?	Tom hid the box before breakfast.
How long?	Tom hid the box for a week.
How often?	Tom hid the box every day.
How?	Tom hid the box by covering it with coats.
Why?	Tom hid the box so Jakie wouldn't find it.
With whom?	Tom hid the box with Joe.

Let's practise!
Underline the verb and circle the adverbial in this sentence.

Alli ran as far as the station.

(1) Read the question, then read it again. What are you being asked to do? — **Underline the verb and circle the adverbial.**

(2) Find the verb and circle it. — **Alli ran – so ran is the verb.**

(3) What are you told about how she ran? — **We are told where she ran – as far as the station. The adverbial is as far as the station.**

(4) Underline the verb and circle the adverbial. — **Alli ran as far as the station.**

1 Adverbials give the reader more information. Think about extra information that would interest your audience.
2 If an adverbial starts the sentence, it is followed by a comma.

Now try these questions:

1 Circle the verbs and underline the adverbials in these sentences.
a) Jain sat with her legs crossed.
b) The fan worked to cool the air.
c) After the meal, Sam slept.
d) When it rained, the children ran inside.
e) Molly knocked because she wanted to come in.

(1 mark for each line)

/5

2 Write **where? when? how long? how often? how? why? with whom?** after each sentence to show the question each adverbial answers.
a) The plants died because there was a drought. _____
b) Kali worked for three hours. _____
c) Isidore whistled through his front teeth. _____
d) A tree grew on the mountainside. _____
e) Before the holiday, they had to pack. _____
f) Every week, Aiden went to scouts. _____

(1 mark each)

/6

3 Write these sentences adding an adverbial that answers the question at the end.
a) The cat purred. **Why?** _____
b) The building collapsed. **When?** _____
c) Lucy Mae practised the piano. **How often?**
_____
d) Barti went to the park. **With whom?**
_____
e) Renata worked. **How?** _____

(1 mark for each line)

/5

4 Write a sentence containing each adverbial. Make sure that the adverbial is telling you more about the verb.
a) at the weekend _____
b) by the canal _____
c) every three hours _____
d) to check how well we were doing
_____
e) for a fortnight _____

(1 mark for each line)

/5

CHALLENGE Try using connectives to start adverbials. How many different connectives can you find that will work?

Embedded clauses

Definitions: Embedded clauses are clauses that are in the middle of a sentence – as if they are tucked up in bed! They are separated from the rest of the sentence, usually by commas.

To make a sentence with an embedded clause:

1 Write a simple sentence: The boy jumped up.

2 Think about some extra information about the boy (perhaps what he looked like or what he was doing apart from jumping up).
He was wearing pyjamas.   He was watching a film.   He had freckles.

3 Choose the information you are going to use and make it into a clause starting with which or who: who was watching a film

4 Put the clause in the middle of sentence, with a comma before and after it:
The boy, who was watching the film, jumped up.

Let's practise!
Put the commas in this sentence to show the embedded clause.

The door which was the only way out was locked.

1	Read the question, then read it again. What are you being asked to do?	**Put the commas in the sentence to show the embedded clause.**
2	Think what the sentence says.	**It is telling us about the door.**
3	Look at the beginning and end of the sentence to find the simple sentence.	**The beginning says** The door **and the end tells us it was locked, so the simple sentence is** The door was locked.
4	Look what else the sentence says.	**It also says** which was the only way out **so this is the embedded clause.**
5	Put a comma before and after the embedded clause.	The door, which was the only way out, was locked.

TOP TIP
Commas can change the meaning of a sentence.
Boys who are energetic like dodge-ball.
This tells us that only energetic boys like dodge-ball.
Boys, who are energetic, like dodge-ball.
This tells us that all boys are energetic and like dodge-ball.
TOP TIP

Now try these questions:

1 Underline the embedded clause in each of these sentences.
a) The umbrella, which was new, blew inside out.
b) The drink, which was too hot, burned Lani's mouth.
c) Joe, who wasn't holding the handlebars, fell off his bike.
d) The school play, which was superb, was called Let's Get Away!
e) Isabella, who was reading, got told off for not listening.

(1 mark each)

/5

2 Put the commas in these sentences to show the embedded clauses.
a) The art lesson which lasted for one hour involved modelling.
b) Assemblies which we have every day are too long.
c) Truck drivers who often have to drive all day have to take regular rest breaks.
d) The farmer who needed to harvest his hay watched the weather forecast.
e) Robert who was frightened ran into the house.

(1 mark for each line)

/5

3 Tick the sentences that are written correctly. If the sentence is incorrect, explain why.
a) Eleanor who likes, to learn, has a fantastic smile.
_____
b) The chair, which was cracked, broke when I sat down.
_____
c) These bananas, they are all green, are not ripe.
_____
d) Mrs Butcher, best teacher ever, taught us English.
_____
e) The children, who were bored, started to throw things.
_____

(1 mark for each line)

/5

4 Make these simple sentences complex by inserting an embedded clause.
a) The house is old. _____
b) The car is new. _____
c) Children like telling jokes. _____
d) Petrol is very expensive. _____
e) William likes using the robots. _____

(1 mark for each line)

/5

CHALLENGE Write as many sentences with embedded clauses as you can where removing the commas leaves a complete sentence with a different meaning.
Can you see a pattern in your answers?

Connectives and cohesion

Purpose: **Connectives** link together ideas in one sentence or between different sentences and paragraphs. Linking ideas and sentences gives your writing **cohesion** – it holds it together and gives it more meaning.

Connectives can be grouped into different types, according to their function in the sentence. Look at the types and the example given for each:

Qualifying connectives	Illustrating connectives	Contrasting connectives	Adding connectives
although	such as	alternatively	also
Comparing connectives	**Cause and effect connectives**	**Emphasising connectives**	**Sequencing connectives**
likewise	so	in particular	finally

Let's practise!

Choose suitable connectives to join these sentences. You may want to change some of the words and word orders.

a) The boys teased the girls. They got into trouble.

b) Jake likes cars. He likes the Ferrari the best.

1 Read the question, then read it again. What are you being asked to do?

Link the sentences using connectives.

2 How are the first two sentences connected?

The second sentence is caused by what happens first.

3 Select a suitable cause and effect connective.

consequently **links the two sentences:** The boys teased the girls. Consequently, they got into trouble.

4 How are the second two sentences connected?

The second sentence emphasises the first connective.

5 Select a suitable emphasising connective.

especially **links the two sentences:** Jake likes cars, especially the Ferrari.

• BEWARE • BEWARE • BEWARE • BEWARE • BEWARE •

Not all connectives are conjunctions. If they are not conjunctions, they need to be used in a new sentence or with a conjunction in the same sentence. Especially acts as a conjunction, but consequently doesn't.

Now try these questions:

1 **a)** Write these connectives in the correct box in the table.
moreover, for instance, thus, as well as, otherwise, like, eventually, for example, first, consequently, as revealed by, indeed, equally, and, before, as with, significantly, despite, in the case of, next, therefore, after, similarly, whereas, meanwhile, since, above all, instead of, in the same way, unlike, on the other hand, notably, because, too, then, especially

Qualifying connectives although	Illustrating connectives such as	Contrasting connectives alternatively	Adding connectives also
Comparing connectives likewise	**Cause and effect connectives** so	**Emphasising connectives** in particular	**Sequencing connectives** finally

(1 mark for every 6 in boxes and 1 mark for every 2 highlighted)

/33

b) Highlight the connectives in the table that could be used as conjunctions.

2 Make the most suitable matches between the different parts of the sentence.

First part of the sentence	Connectives with conjunctions	Second part of the sentence
I peeled the vegetables	so, consequently,	Max lit the fire.
I was late	and, meanwhile,	someone answered the door.
I kept pressing the bell	until, eventually,	I missed the bus.
Everyone went on the trip	as well as	today was his birthday.
I did the shopping	especially as	cleaning the house.
I finished my work	except	lunchtime.
William was happy,	during	the boys who broke the window.

(1 mark for each line)

/7

CHALLENGE Write a paragraph using a variety of connectives to give your writing cohesion.

21

I and Me

Definition: Words that refer to yourself.

> I went to the football match.

> Show me how to do that!

The problem: When you talk about yourself with another person it can be tricky to know whether to use I or me.

> You and I went skating.

> You and me went skating.

The solution: Try the sentence just for yourself.

> I went skating.

> Me went skating.

Now it is easy to see which is correct – and that tells you which you need to use, so the correct sentence is:

> You and I went skating.

Let's practise!

Fill the blank correctly in this sentence using I or me.

The teacher gave the box to John and [＿＿＿].

1	Read the question, then read it again. What are you being asked to do?	**Work out whether I or me is the correct word to use in the sentence.**
2	Take the additional person out of the sentence.	The teacher gave the box to _____ .
3	Test the sentence using I and me.	The teacher gave the box to I. The teacher gave the box to me.
4	Choose the option which sounds correct.	The teacher gave the box to me.
5	Put your answer into the original sentence.	The teacher gave the box to John and me.

TOP TIP Remember to test the sentence as if it is just about yourself. **TOP TIP**

Now try these questions:

1 Fill in the blanks correctly using I or me.

a) John and _____ jump.

b) He likes Sam and _____ .

c) Look where Alfie and _____ live.

(1 mark each)

/3

2 Tick the sentences that are correct.

Zia and I went fishing.	
Liam came with Conor and me.	
Lani and me ate pizza for dinner.	
They presented a cup to Laura and I.	
If Caitlin and I win, we will share the prize with Nye.	
Don't ask Eleanor and me to do the tidying up!	

(1 mark each)

/6

3 Fill in the blanks correctly using I or me.

a) Jake and _____ went to the disco.

b) The swimming pool is near where Max and _____ went walking.

c) Give the paints to Tom and _____ so we can finish our model.

d) Why do you and _____ always get the blame?

e) Thanks to you and _____ , that went really well.

(1 mark each)

/5

4 Fill in the blanks with either me or I, so that the sentence is correct.

a) My friend and _____ are here.

b) Why do you always blame Xia and _____?

c) Sam and _____ have finished.

d) Do you see the same problem as Cydney and _____ do?

e) Don't forget about Stephi and _____ .

(1 mark each)

/5

CHALLENGE

Make a set of ten cards with sentences using I and me. Make five of them correct and five incorrect. Challenge your friends and family to sort them.

Formal writing and Standard English

Definition: Standard English is English that follows accepted rules of grammar and that many people believe to be 'correct'. It is usual to use Standard English in formal situations.

Some rules to consider:

- Always use complete sentences.
- Try to avoid starting sentences with a conjunction.
- Try to avoid ending a sentence with a preposition.
- Make sure tenses are correct.
- Make sure subjects and verbs agree.
- Write in the third person (use one instead of you).
- Avoid double negatives, contractions and abbreviations.
- Avoid idioms, figurative language and colloquialisms (words in informal conversations).
- Use precise and technical language
- Be as objective as possible

Let's practise!

Rewrite this sentence using Standard English.

> So he'd chucked it out of window 'cos he don't know nobody were under.

1	Read the question, then read it again. What are by being asked to do?	**Change the passage to Standard English.**
2	Check that the sentence is complete, doesn't start with a conjunction and doesn't end with a preposition.	He'd **chucked it out of the window 'cos he didn't know that** underneath **were nobody.**
3	Check the person, tenses and subject–verb agreement.	He'd **chucked it out of the window 'cos he didn't know that underneath there** was **nobody.**
4	Remove double negatives, contractions and abbreviations.	He had **chucked it out of the window** because **he** did not **know that underneath there was somebody.**
5	Remove idioms, figurative language and colloquialisms.	He had thrown **it out of the window because he did not know that underneath there was somebody.**
6	Check that the writing is formal and the vocabulary is precise and technical.	He had thrown it out of the window because he **did not know that** a person was underneath.

Now try these questions:

1 Rewrite these sentences formally.

a) Give us one of them sweets.

_____

b) He should of been as sick as a parrot.

_____

c) Me brother learned me to play the drums.

_____

d) What did you do that for?

_____

(2 marks each)

e) There isn't no pencils in the cupboard.

_____

/14

f) Can I have a lend of your stuff?

_____

g) He should of had a fab day.

_____

2 Rewrite this passage using Standard English.

> I were skiving with me mates on Monday afternoon, when I saw a well cool top. I so wanted it that I dunned one of me mates for the readies he lent from me. Don't know what he did that for. Anyways, I razzed the top and changed me mind 'cos I din't want it no more.

(10 marks)

/10

_____

_____

_____

_____

_____

3 Circle the correct word to complete each sentence.

a) Louise did not eat (nothing / anything) at lunchtime.

b) The tiger could (of / have) deserted its cubs and escaped.

(7 marks)

c) If necessary, pupils can (lend / borrow) items of equipment.

/7

d) All the pupils were (learned / taught) how to cancel fractions.

e) The drink was (well / very) cool.

f) The elephant (does not / don't) like confined spaces.

g) The document will be ready (soon as / as soon as) possible.

CHALLENGE Find a piece of formal writing and rewrite it informally.

Speech

By Level 5 you need to be expert at punctuating speech. Let's review the basic rules.

Rules for punctuating speech:

> 1 Put " " around what the speaker says.
>
> 2 A new speech sentence starts with a capital letter (even if it is in the middle of another sentence).
>
> 3 Separate what was said from the speaker with a comma unless there is already a ? or an !
>
> 4 Start a new paragraph if a new speaker says something.

At Level 5 you should also be able to apply these speech rules:

> 5 When quoting another speaker in direct speech, use single inverted commas: "I asked where she was going but she said, 'Mind your own business'," I told them.
>
> 6 Only put a capital letter after the first speech marks if it's the start of a speech sentence: "Well," complained Georgia, "she didn't have to say it like that." Notice that the she at the start of the second speech mark does not have a capital letter because it is not the start of the speech sentence.

Let's practise!
Punctuate the speech in this sentence correctly.

> anyway said Evie why did she shout go away like that?

1 Read the question, then read it again. What are you being asked to do?

Punctuate the speech in the sentence.

2 Work out exactly what was said and put " " around the words.

Evie said: anyway why did she shout go away like that? **So we write:** "anyway" said Evie "why did she shout go away like that?"

3 Start the speech sentence with a capital letter and separate the speech from the speaker with commas.

"Anyway," said Evie, "why did she shout go away like that?"

4 Check if there is a quotation in the speech.

Yes – someone shouted "go away".

5 Put single inverted commas around the quote, start the speech sentence with a capital letter and use commas to separate the quote from the rest of the sentence.

"Anyway," said Evie, "why did she shout, 'Go away,' like that?" **If 'Go away,' was shouted it needs to end with an exclamation mark.** "Anyway," said Evie, "why did she shout, 'Go away!' like that?"

Now try these questions:

1 Put the capital letters and speech punctuation in the correct place in these sentences.

a) watch this whispered mark. he's going to open the cupboard door.

b) if intoned mr pattison i hear anyone say, it's not fair, i will be very upset.

c) stop called the policeman or i will arrest you.

d) he is stated kerry a very silly boy.

(1 mark for each line)

/4

2 Circle the errors in this speech punctuation.

a) "Don't worry said Pat, we'll find it."

b) "Perhaps," mused Andy, You could make more of an effort."

c) "Tom said, "I'm coming," but I told him he couldn't", confessed Barti.

d) "If Lani said that Rob said that you said I don't want to go, then I believe her," said Ruby.

(1 mark for each line)

/4

3 Rewrite this paragraph, punctuating it correctly.

> When the weather is sunny said Max its good to go out. It's good to go out anyway retorted Rowan. Yes agreed Isidore because my mum said if you stay in the house any longer I think I'll go mad and she did look like she was losing it. Yes said Rowan and I think my mum has the same problem.

(6 marks)

/6

4 Tick the sentences that are correctly punctuated.

	Is it correct?	If no, explain why not.
"Sit up," said the teacher, "And look this way."		
"Mum said, "No, you can't!"" said Eleanor.		
"Let's rest," suggested George, "before we walk any further."		
"Well, she was surprised. 'Never mind' I told her – you can't win them all!" laughed Nan.		
"Rest," ordered John, "before you do any more work."		
"Two weeks," I informed him, "So don't say, 'no-one told me,' because I'm telling you now."		

(2 marks each)

/12

CHALLENGE Write a dialogue that illustrates all the rules of speech.

Commas

You should already know how to use commas in these ways:

- to separate speech from the speaker (if no other punctuation is used)
- to separate items in a list (replacing the word and or or)
- after extra information is added at the start of a sentence (a fronted adverbial).

Other uses of the comma include:

- before the words and, or, but, yet or while when they join two sentences:
  The rehearsal is tomorrow, but I have my induction day at high school then.
- to separate extra information in the sentence (usually used in pairs):
  Matthew, during playtime, banged his head.
- to separate the name or title of the person being directly addressed:
  "Will you, Abnir, go and fetch the technology trolley?"
- to separate a question from a statement: You will come, won't you?

Let's practise!

Put commas where they are needed in this sentence:

> Jaquin took the long difficult path which was very steep all the way to the top but I didn't.

1	Read the question, then read it again. What are you being asked to do?	**Put the commas into the sentence**
2	Check if there is any speech.	**No**
3	Check if there is a list.	Long difficult path. **Could they be separated by and? Yes – long and difficult path – so put a comma between them.**
4	Check if there is extra information added.	Which was very steep **could be removed from the sentence, so put commas before and after it.**
5	Check for the words and, or, but, yet and while then check if there are complete sentences before and after them.	**Yes – the word** but **is used and there is a complete sentence before and after it, so use a comma before it.**
6	Is there a question and a statement? Or is someone being directly addressed?	**No**
7	Write your answer with the commas.	Jaquin took the long, difficult path, which was very steep, all the way to the top, but I didn't.

Now try these questions:

1 Tick the sentences where the commas are used correctly.
a) Imogen, Vanessa and Jonathan, who live in Wales, keep hens.
b) She wanted to do her homework, as well as go to the park, to play.
c) When I laugh, it makes me sneeze, if I have hay fever.
d) Only yesterday, Olivia was making a theatre when, unfortunately it broke.
e) After tea, we watched a video, which was extremely funny, until it was time to leave.

(1 mark for each line)

/5

2 In each box, write an **E** if the comma separates extra information from the sentence; an **L** if it is used in a list; a **J** if it is used before **and**, **or**, **but**, **yet** or **while** to join two sentences.

a) The monster, which breathed poisonous gas, turned to me.

b) The shop, which was tiny, sold papers, drinks and snacks, and we bought the lot!

(1 mark each)

/6

3 Check the commas in these sentences. Tick them if they are correct and rewrite them correctly if they are not.
a) Andy, trying to be helpful, piled up the boots coats and hats.

b) Whilst reading a story I noticed the window, was open.

c) "You can do that can't you?," asked Lisa.

d) The eagle, soaring overhead, scanned the area, hunting prey.

e) I do well in maths, reading, and science but I do best in writing.

(1 mark for each line)

/5

4 Put commas where they are needed in these sentences.
a) Annie received money books and toys for her birthday which was yesterday.
b) Alli pleaded "Please James you will play won't you?"

(1 mark for each line)

/2

CHALLENGE Write the title The journey on a piece of paper or in your book. Write sentences linked to the title, using commas in all the ways shown in this section. Your writing can be factual or fictional.

Semi-colons

Using semi-colons correctly can improve your writing.

A semi-colon is used to separate two complete sentences that are very closely related but should not be joined with a colon. For example:

In winter the snow was freezing cold; in summer the sun was blazing hot.

There needs to be a complete sentence both before and after the semi-colon, but don't use a capital letter for the second sentence.

Let's practise!
Match the first half of the sentence to the most appropriate second half.

Tegan ran down the hill;

which was lots of fun.
Whitney walked up it.
it was too steep to walk down.

1 Read the question, then read it again. What are you being asked to do?

Choose the best ending to complete the sentence.

2 Think what the first part of the sentence says.

It tells us about Tegan.

3 Think why there is a semi-colon at the end of it.

Semi-colons separate two sentences that are closely related.

4 Check the options for the second part of the sentence.

It must be a full sentence, so it can't be which was lots of fun because that isn't a full sentence.

5 What are the other two endings?

They are both full sentences. The first is about how Whitney moved on the hill. The other tells us why Tegan ran down the hill.

6 Decide which cold be used after a semi-colon.

Whitney walked up it. Is related because it contrasts the movement on the hill. It could be used after a semi-colon. It was too steep to walk down. This explains the first sentence, so it should be separated from it by a colon.
Tegan ran down the hill; Whitney walked up it.

Only use a semi-colon if you can't use a colon.

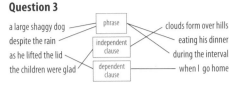

Answers

Page 7 Word classes

Question 1 a) noun, verb **b)** adjective, adverb
c) noun, verb, adjective **d)** noun, verb, adjective
e) noun, verb

Question 2

Suddenly,	we	saw	a
adverb	pronoun	verb	article
shape	emerge	from	the
noun	verb	preposition	article
shadows.			
noun			

The	dogs	howled	because
article	noun	verb	connective / conjunction
of	the	fireworks.	
preposition	article	noun	

Eat	healthy	foods	while
verb	adjective	noun	connective
you	are	growing.	
pronoun	verb	verb	

Although	it	is	cold,
connective	pronoun	verb	adjective
I	am	going.	
pronoun	verb	verb	

Question 3 Answers will vary. Sample answers:

Consequently,	the	lazy	dog
connective	article	adjective	noun
grew	fatter.		
verb	adverb		

Mice	hide	quietly	under
noun	verb	adverb	preposition
the	sofa	all	day.
article	noun	adjective	noun

An	honest	man	pays
article	adjective	noun	verb
while	you	unlawfully	steal.
connective	pronoun	adverb	verb

Challenge Answers will vary. Sample answers:
Nouns: proper, common, countable, uncountable, mass, collective, concrete, abstract, pronouns

Verbs: auxillary, lexical, dynamic, stative, finite, non-finite, regular, irregular, transitive, intransitive, causative

Adverb: place, time, manner, degree, quantity, frequency, affirmative, negation, interrogation, relative

Page 9 Nouns
Question 1

Abstract nouns	Collective nouns	Common nouns	Proper nouns	Uncountable nouns
art	army	bag	London	art
health	company	chair	Uncle	health
weather	family	clarinet	Gary	weather
electricity	audience	bus	Harry	electricity
advice		furniture	New York	advice
bravery			English	happiness
curiosity				trust
fear				(abstract
happiness				nouns are
trust				usually
freedom				uncountable)

Question 2 a) Charlotte's, anger, work, chocolate
b) bunch, flowers, Miss Lomas's embarrassment
c) Harvey, help, homework, Rio **d)** greed, children, problem, everyone **e)** school council, agreement, Mrs Hartley, playground equipment

Question 3 a) bevy **b)** herd / memory / parade
c) colony / army / swarm **d)** gaggle **e)** litter
f) pride **g)** lodge / colony **h)** parliament **i)** murder
j) school / herd

Question 4 a) My first school was called Gleadless Primary School. **b)** The best book about cats is called The Cat Kingdom. **c)** My favourite uncle is Uncle Tom. **d)** At Headless Cross there is thought to be a headless ghost. **e)** Whaley Memorial Park is a fantastic park to visit.

Challenge Answers will vary. Sample answer may include: water, air, wood, cheese, snow, happiness, loneliness, freedom, fun, work, travel, sleep, information, understanding

Page 11 Subject, object and verb

Question 1 a) The owl hoots. **b)** A lady screamed.
c) The children were skipping. **d)** The bus stopped.
e) They are busy. **f)** The fire-engine is red.

Question 2

sentence	subject	object	predicate
The man washed the car.	man	car	washed
The trees were uprooted by the wind.	trees	wind	uprooted
Over the sea, the ship was sailing.	ship	sea	sailing
The traffic jam went through Manchester.	traffic jam	Manchester	went
Across the lawn danced the fairies.	fairies	lawn	danced

Question 3 a) object **b)** subject **c)** object **d)** subject
e) subject

Question 4 Answers will vary. **a)** subject, e.g. She
b) verb, e.g. missing **c)** subject, e.g. they

Challenge Compound subjects = more than one subject. For example: Peter, Paul and Imran went out. Compound verbs = the subject does more than one thing. For example: I peeled the vegetables and sliced the meat. We laughed and sang all day.

Page 13 Active and passive sentences
Question 1

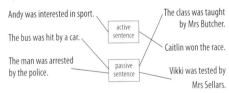

Question 2 a) P **b)** A **c)** P **d)** A

Question 3 a) The children had eaten the cake.
b) The infants were spoiling the game. **c)** The audience appreciated the play. **d)** The snow is hiding the plants.

Question 4 a) Harvey is being chased by James.
b) Skye is being laughed at by Megan. **c)** Ms Wright is being helped by Mrs Mellor.

Challenge Answers will vary. A comment could be that there are few passive voice sentences because they are harder to read and understand.

Page 15 Phrases and clauses
Question 1 a) C **b)** C **c)** P **d)** C **e)** P **f)** C **g)** C **h)** C

Question 2 a) The dog whined when it heard the fireworks. **b)** Because it was snowing, we built a large snowman. **c)** We were allowed cake since it was my birthday. **d)** Reece fell down so we had to abandon the race. **e)** When Louie was away, we did a maths test.

Question 3

a large shaggy dog	→	clouds form over hills
despite the rain	phrase	eating his dinner
as he lifted the lid	independent clause	during the interval
the children were glad	dependent clause	when I go home

Question 4 a) Whilst watching the match, Sonal started to feel ill. **b)** The forest was dark and gloomy; the mountains were light and airy. **c)** The phone rang just as tea was ready. **d)** When he saw the bill, Sam was very cross.

Question 5 Answers will vary. Sample answers:
a) While it was raining, we played indoors. **b)** Serena played on her computer, after she finished her homework. **c)** I took my jumper off because it was hot.

Challenge Answers will vary. Which list is longest will depend on the type, complexity and style of text. Simple fiction will have more independent clauses because it uses less complex sentence structures. This is a chance for pupils to look at and evaluate a text while reflecting on the intended audience.

Page 17 Adverbs and adverbials

Question 1 a) Jain sat with her legs crossed. **b)** The fan worked to cool the air. **c)** After the meal, Sam slept. **c)** When it rained, the children ran inside. **d)** Molly knocked because she wanted to come in.

Question 2 a) why? **b)** how long? **c)** how? **d)** where?
e) when? **f)** how often?

Question 3 Answers will vary. Sample answers:
a) The cat purred because she was content. **b)** The building collapsed last week. **c)** Lucy Mae practised the piano every day. **d)** Barti went to the park with his mates. **e)** Renata worked long and hard.

Question 4 Answers will vary. Sample answers:
a) I am going to the park at the weekend. **b)** Sian is going for a walk by the canal. **c)** Make sure you take your medicine every three hours. **d)** Mum looked in to check how well we were doing. **e)** They are going on holiday for a fortnight.

Challenge Answers will vary. Connectives that might start adverbials include:

comparison	as though
condition	if, as long as, provided that
contrast	however, although, whereas, even though
purpose	so, in order to
reason	because, since, as, consequently, hence, therefore
time	after, before, as soon as

Page 19 Embedded clauses

Question 1 a) which was new **b)** which was too hot
c) who wasn't holding the handlebars **d)** which was superb **e)** who was reading

Question 2 a) The art lesson, which lasted for one hour, involved modelling. **b)** Assemblies, which we have every day, are too long. **c)** Truck drivers, who often have to drive all day, have to take regular rest breaks. **d)** The farmer, who needed to harvest his hay, watched the weather forecast. **e)** Robert, who was frightened, ran into the house.

Question 3 a) No – the first comma is incorrectly placed. **b)** ✔ **c)** No – there is a sentence in the place of the embedded clause. **d)** No – the embedded clause is not complete. **e)** ✔

Question 4 Answers will vary. Check the embedded clause and commas are correct. Sample answers: **a)** The house, which is down the road, is old. **b)** The car, which Dad has bought, is new. **c)** Children, who are funny, like telling jokes. **d)** Petrol, that makes some cars run, is very expensive. **e)** William, who enjoys electronic toys, likes using the robots.

Challenge Answers will vary. Pattern could be that plural nouns often work with and without commas.

Page 21 Connectives and cohesion

Questions 1 a) and 1 b)

Qualifying connectives	Illustrating connectives
although, however, unless, despite, except, if, as long as	such as, for example, for instance, as revealed by, in the case of
Contrasting connectives	**Adding connectives**
alternatively, whereas, instead of, otherwise, unlike,	also, moreover, and, as well as, too
Comparing connectives	**Cause and effect connectives**
likewise, equally, in the same way, similarly, as with, like	so, because, therefore, thus, consequently, since
Emphasising connectives	**Sequencing connectives**
in particular, especially, above all, significantly, indeed, notably	finally, next, then, first, meanwhile, eventually, after, before

Question 2

I peeled the vegetables	so, consequently,	Max lit the fire.
I was late	and, meanwhile,	someone answered the door.
I kept pressing the bell	until, eventually,	I missed the bus.
Everyone went on the trip	as well as	today was his birthday.
I did the shopping	especially as	cleaning the house.
I finished my work	except	lunchtime.
William was happy,	during	the boys who broke the window.

Challenge Answers will vary.

Page 23 I and me

Question 1 a) I **b)** me **c)** I

Question 2

Zia and I went fishing.	✔
Liam came with Conor and me.	✔
Lani and me ate pizza for dinner.	
They presented a cup to Laura and I.	
If Caitlin and I win, we will share the prize with Nye.	✔
Don't ask Eleanor and me to do the tidying up!	✔

Question 3 a) I **b)** I **c)** me **d)** I **e)** me

Question 4 a) I **b)** me **c)** I **d)** I **e)** me

Challenge Answers will vary. Sample answer: During the day, whilst Pat did the chores, I continued writing. Despite the lure of the sun, I persisted until, eventually, I completed the task. Whenever I remember that time, I shudder.

Page 25 Formal writing and Standard English

Question 1 a) Give me one of those sweets. **b)** He should have been ill. **c)** My brother taught me to play the drums. **d)** Why did you do that? **e)** There are no pencils in the cupboard. **f)** Can I borrow your equipment / belongings? **g)** He should have had a fabulous day.

Question 2 Answers will vary. Give 2 marks verb–subject agreement, 2 marks correct pronouns, 2 marks correctly structured sentences, 4 marks slang corrected. Sample answer: I took a day away from school on Monday afternoon, when I saw an excellent top. I wanted the top, so demanded that a friend return the money he had borrowed from me for some unspecified purpose. I looked closely at the top and decided against buying it.

Question 3 a) anything **b)** have **c)** borrow **d)** taught **e)** very **f)** does not **g)** as soon as

Challenge Answers will vary.

Page 27 Speech

Question 1 a) "Watch this," whispered Mark. "He's going to open the cupboard door." **b)** "If," intoned Mr Pattison, "I hear anyone say, 'It's not fair,' I will be very upset." **c)** "Stop!" called the policeman, "or I will arrest you." (Or may have a capital letter.) **d)** "He is," stated Kerry, "a very silly boy."

Question 2 a) "Don't worry, said Pat, we'll find it." **b)** "Perhaps," mused Andy, You could make more of an effort." **c)** "Tom said, "I'm coming," but I told him he couldn't, confessed Barti. **d)** "If Lani said that Rob said that you said, I don't want to go, then I believe her," said Ruby.

Question 3 Give 2 marks for correctly placed speech marks, 2 marks for starting a new line for each new speaker, 2 marks for punctuation within speech marks (capital or not and punctuation before second " for each pair).

"When the weather is sunny," said Max, "it's good to go out."

"It's good to go out anyway!" retorted Rowan.

"Yes," agreed Isidore, "because my mum said, 'If you stay in the house any longer I think I'll go mad,' and she did look like she was losing it."

"Yes," said Rowan, "and I think my mum has the same problem!"

Question 4

	Is it correct?	If no, explain why not.
"Sit up," said the teacher, "And look this way."		A capital letter on 'And' which is the middle of the speech sentence.
"Mum said, "No, you can't!" " said Eleanor.		Double inverted commas used for the quote.
"Let's rest," suggested George, "before we walk any further."	✔	
"Well, she was surprised. 'Never mind' I told her – you can't win them all!" laughed Nan.		Needs a comma after 'mind'.
"Rest," ordered John, "before you do any more work."	✔	
"Two weeks," I informed him, "So don't say, 'no-one told me,' because I'm telling you now."		A capital letter on 'So' which is the middle of the speech sentence.

Challenge Answers will vary. Sample answer: "She ordered us to 'Watch and learn!' so we did," laughed Tom.
"What happened?" asked Lucy curiously.
"Well," he replied, "she jumped on one side of the boat and fell straight off the other!"

Page 29 Commas

Question 1 a) ✔ **b)** N **c)** N **d)** N **e)** ✔

Question 2 a) E, E **b)** E, E, L, J

Question 3 a) Andy, trying to be helpful, piled up the boots, coats and hats. **b)** Whilst reading a story, I noticed the window was open. **c)** "You can do that, can't you?" asked Lisa. **d)** ✔ **e)** I do well in maths, reading and science, but I do best in writing.

Question 4 a) Annie received money, books and toys for her birthday, which was yesterday. b) Alli pleaded, "Please, James, you will play, won't you?"

Challenge Answers will vary.

Page 31 Semi-colons

Question 1 a) Cars are a major problem; parking cars can be an even bigger problem. **b)** The book was interesting; the film was really boring. **c)** Eleanor could run for hours; Isobel preferred to ride her bike. **d)** It was hot in the valley; up in the hills it was cool.

Question 2

The maths test was easy;	Carol was the worst.
Joshua was the best player;	Nye liked vegetables.
Andy was very cross;	the reading test was hard.
George liked meat;	Mr Lomas wasn't bothered.
Azim enjoyed reading;	Lekh enjoyed making models.

Question 3 c)

Question 4 Answers will vary. Check each answer is a full sentence and related to the first part of the sentence, but not giving more information about it. Sample answers: **a)** Beth liked going shopping; Stephanie liked to stay at home. **b)** Zak went to bed early; Max stayed up late. **c)** The dragon flew gracefully over the lake; I rowed with all my might to get across. **d)** Exercise helps to keep you healthy; watching television helps keep you entertained.

Question 5 Answers will vary. Check each answer is a full sentence and related to the second part of the sentence, but not giving more information about it. Sample answers: **a)** Joe went to scouts; Caitlin spent the evening reading. **b)** Isidore mended the bed; Billy mended the model. **c)** Dad took them up a mountain; Barti wanted to go to the seaside. **d)** Jake liked music; Gill could play the piano.

Challenge Answers will vary. Sample answers: **a)** The semi-colon can be used to link sentences which use conjunction connectors. These are words like otherwise, however, therefore, moreover, nevertheless, thus, besides, accordingly, consequently, instead, hence. **b)** Use the semi-colon to separate items in a list when one or more items contain a comma.

Page 33 Colons

Question 1 a) The children didn't finish their work: they had spent too much time talking. **b)** The box was heavy: it was full of old books. **c)** Cydney was worried: she hadn't seen Charlie for two days. **d)** There was a loud bang: the wall collapsed.

Question 2

Andy was a good coach:	he had studied every night.
Joshua was the best player:	he spent an hour on it every night.
Max wanted to pass the exam:	he went to the library every week.
George liked his computer:	he made Lori train properly.
Azim enjoyed reading:	he was the team captain.

Pull out these eight pages so that you can use them easily to help you learn and practise your spelling.

HOW TO PREPARE FOR THE SPELLING TEST

(1) Keep a list of the words that you can spell as well as those you need to work on. Don't spend time working on the words you can already spell!

(2) Do spelling learning somewhere you can work without distractions – so not in front of the television!

(3) If you like to learn by doing things, use cards, magnets and plastic letters that you can move around to spell words; write spellings in sand; write on the playground with chalk; use finger paints to spell words; type spellings onto a computer (without the spell check!); and use objects associated with the words wherever possible.

(4) If you learn well by hearing things, say the words as you look at them; practise saying words in the way they are spelled (for example, j-ud-g-ed); use the words you have to learn when you are talking; and make tricky spellings into songs, such as using the tune to Twinkle, Twinkle Little Star:

Phys-i -cal -ly – I must spell
I can do it very well
P – h – y – s – i – c – a
l – l – y that is the way
P – h – y – s – i - c – a
l – l – y that is the way

(5) If you learn by seeing things, close your eyes and 'see' the word; use flashcards with the vowels and consonants in different colours – perhaps with important letter strings highlighted; copy the word many times; read lots of books (if you have read a word more than 30 times you will have a good idea how it is spelled); use a book to hunt for the words you learning to spell; and think of words that look similar.

(6) If you are a cognitive (thinking) learner, you are probably already a good speller, but you can use all of the ideas for other learners to help with the tricky words!

(7) Learn with friends:
- Throw a small ball to each other, spelling out the word with one letter for each catch. Help by correcting each other's spelling when needed.
- Have sets of letter cards and race to put the letters in order for the word you need to spell, or race to write the words (legibly) on a whiteboard.
- Create board games that quiz you on the words you are learning.
- Race each other to text the word correctly, or to type it on the computer.

(8) Of course, use look, say, cover, write, check.

(9) Practise little and often for really effective learning. Five minutes of practice a day will help you more than half-an-hour's work just before a test.

(10) Remember, you are learning to spell to communicate effectively as an adult in a competitive world. Don't be the one who is rejected because of poor spelling – and, yes, that does happen!

Tricky words

Some words are tricky to spell and these are worth spending some extra time looking at. All the example words have been used in SAT spelling tests!

(1) Words that use a **c** for an **s** sound.
For example: **audience, exciting, silence, centre**

(2) Nouns that use **c** when the verb uses an **s**.
For example: **advice/advise, practice/practise, device/devise**

(3) Words with silent letters.
For example: **environment, interesting, strength, designed**

(4) Words that end in **–al**
For example: **special, digital, individual, festival**

(5) Words that end in the **–shun** sound
For example: **destination, invention, pollution**

(6) Words using the **–ough** word string.
For example: **throughout, thoroughly**

Unstressed vowels: shwa

stationary

poisonous

separate

affectionate

boundary

acoustics

apologies

suspicion

original

anonymous

Silent vowels and syllables

average

nation

generally

answer

Wednesday

January

mortgage

campaign

whistle

muscle

Other ways of spelling /sh/: **cial**

crucial

especially

artificial

financial

antisocial

officially

beneficial

judicial

sacrificial

superficial

Unstressed vowels: shwa

frightening

specialist

secretary

general

nuisance

literature

dictionary

recreational

jewellery

neighbourhood

Same pronunciation, different spelling /sh/

outpatient

quotient

ancient

efficient

proficient

coefficient

crustacean

compassion

tissue

reissue

Suffixes: **ant**

hesitate – hesitant

observe – observant

resist – resistant

contest – contestant

participate – participant

abundance – abundant

signify – significant

dominate – dominant

account – accountant

tolerate – tolerant

Suffixes: **ation**

pronounce – pronunciation

interpret – interpretation

exasperate – exasperation

consider – consideration

separate – separation

desolate – desolation

imagine – imagination

vary – variation

accuse – accusation

category – categorisation

ough

enough

cough

although

breakthrough

thoughtless

besought

snowplough

thorough

bought

drought

Hyphenated words

co-ordination

re-iteration

co-operative

pre-eminent

re-alignment

all-inclusive

self-assured

mid-July

ninety-eight

bad-tempered

Suffixes: **ancy, ency, cies**

proficient – proficiencies

emerge – emergency

absorb – absorbency

infant – infancy

truant – truancy

vacant – vacancies

conserve – conservancy

decent – decency

lenient – leniency

depend – dependencies

Exceptions to **i** before **e**

heiress

abseil

airfreight

perceive

feigned

weird

forfeit

deign

protein

leisure

Suffixes: **ate**

assimilate

articulate

appropriate

fascinate

concentrate

speculate

inaccurate

frustrate

celebrate

exaggerate

Suffixes: **or, er**

spectacle – spectator
compete – competitor
assess – assessor
legislate – legislator
success – successor
achieve – achiever
control – controller
engine – engineer
laugh – laughter
photocopy – photocopier

Suffixes: **ary, ory**

contributory
obligatory
sensory
laboratory
introductory
advisory
unnecessary
vocabulary
cautionary
voluntary

Suffixes: **ent, ment**

advertise – advertisement
commit – commitment
appear – apparent
argue – argument
indulge – indulgent
concur – concurrent
descend – descendent
suffice – sufficient
require – requirement
serve – servient

Suffixes: **ible** and **able**

audible
fallible
terrible
incomprehensible
responsible
reliable
applicable
impressionable
preferable
incapable

Suffixes: **ible** and **able**

rely – reliable
value – valuable
change – changeable
deplore – deplorable
achieve – achievable
convert – convertible
intelligent – intelligible
sense – sensible
response – responsible
digest – digestible

Sound similar

affect – effect
eligible – illegible
ascent – assent
principal – principle
allusion – illusion
precede – proceed
desert – dessert
compliment – complement
advice – advise
assistants – assistance

Suffixes: **ance**

annoy – annoyance

grieve – grievance

rely – reliance

ignore – ignorance

comply – compliance

hinder – hindrance

maintain – maintenance

important – importance

repent – repentance

assure – assurance

Suffixes: **ence**

expert – experience

coincident – coincidence

audio – audience

obedient – obedience

persist – persistence

sense – sentence

exist – existence

confident – confidence

impatient – impatience

insist – insistence

Suffixes: **tial**

essential

substantial

preferential

impartial

potential

celestial

influential

providential

circumstantial

consequential

Suffixes: **ious**

infect – infectious

anxiety – anxious

fiction – fictitious

malice – malicious

glory – glorious

conscience – conscientious

caution – cautious

rebel – rebellious

suspicion – suspicious

envy – envious

Suffixes: unstressed **ence**

innocent – innocence

intelligent – intelligence

differ – difference

defend – defence

present – presence

excel – excellence

exist – existence

violent – violence

absent – absence

adolescent – adolescence

Plurals with no singular

aircraft

crossroads

trousers

scissors

species

shorts

pyjamas

series

cattle

information

Using meaning to predict spelling

collect – collection
please – pleasure
busy – business
supreme – supremacy
ballet – ballerina
treasure – treasury
tyrant – tyranny
grace – gracious
law – lawyer
nerve – nervous

Silent vowels

casualty
believe
catalogue
manual
heaven
diamond
carriage
fashion
feisty
tongue

Silent vowels

jeopardy
heist
queue
giraffe
vogue
prosperous
building
allegiance
guillotine
villain

Silent **psy, pn, mn, wr, gn**

psychotic
psychopath
psychiatrist
pneumonia
pneumatic
mnemonically
typewritten
wreckage
assignment
foreign

Silent vowels

aisle
people
memorable
library
guidance
biscuit
source
cushion
beautifully
miserable

Useful words list

unusual
regardless
challenging
evidence
triumph
recent
frequently
individual
generation
actually

Useful words list

serious
successful
disguised
lenient
mysterious
harassment
extremely
journey
favour
embarrass

Useful words list

management
particularly
determined
purpose
superior
disturbed
hoax
punctuality
extinguishing
tomorrow

Useful words list

guarantee
journeying
opinion
explanation
sympathetic
genre
credibility
humility
genuine
bribery

Useful words list

qualified
necessary
encounter
parliament
destination
attempt
mischievous
outrageous
whether
century

Useful words list

apprehensive
sincerely
required
encourage
syllable
tyrant
realistic
helpful
European
severity

Unstressed vowels: schwa

separately
aggressive
dissatisfaction
whereabouts
abundance
temperature
equator
illustrator
surveyor
recommended

Question 3 Answers will vary. Check the lists match the opening, that commas are used correctly and that the last two items are joined with and. Sample answers: **a)** jumpers, t-shirts and dresses. **b)** sheep, pigs, chickens and cows. **c)** the roundabout, dodgems and helter skelter. **d)** Sian, Joe, David and Alun.

Question 4 Answers will vary. Check that the second part is a full sentence and explains or illustrates the first sentence. Sample answers: **a)** it didn't finish till late. **b)** she had helped her grandma move house. **c)** the trouble was he didn't want to do it. **d)** they have been known to attack swimmers.

Question 5 Answers will vary. Sample answers: **a)** Ravi was looking forward to his dinner. **b)** The jumper was knitted in my favourite colours. **c)** My best friends are coming to my party. **d)** I go swimming three times a week.

Challenge Answers will vary. Sample answers could include: To introduce a quotation. After the name of a speaker in a play-script.
E.g.: The posters all said: "If you can't stand the heat, get out of the kitchen."
John: (enthusiastically) I'm ready – let's go!

Page 35 Hyphens
Question 1 a) accident-prone **b)** computer-aided **c)** good-looking **d)** sugar-free **e)** power-driven

Question 2

custom-built — built to the customer's specification
ex-husband — man that someone used to be married to
camera-ready — ready to be filmed
self-pity — feeling sorrow for yourself
mayor-elect — the person selected to be the next mayor
all-inclusive — everything paid for

Question 3 Answers will vary. Sample answers: **a)** The quick-thinking girl managed to put out the fire. **b)** The bad-tempered boy wasn't very popular. **c)** The muddle-headed professor mixed up the experiment. **d)** The co-owner of the gym was a fitness instructor. **e)** Seventy-six balloons went up into the sky.

Question 4 a) fifty-five **b)** seventy-one **c)** two-thirds **d)** ninety-eight **e)** twenty-seven **f)** forty-three

Challenge Answers will vary. Sample answers: put-upon – taken advantage of; snarl-up – traffic jam or muddle

Page 37 Ellipsis
Question 1

	Words missed out	A speaker trailed off	To show a pause
The fireman said, " . . . it was started deliberately."	✔		
"I'm not sure . . ." whispered Caitlin.		✔	
Ofsted reported that the children . . . behaved well.	✔		
Rowan waited . . . and waited . . . and waited.			✔
"Please . . . stop it . . . don't . . ." shouted Charlotte.			✔
"I wonder . . ." said Mrs Butcher.		✔	

Question 2 a) to show words are missed out **b)** to show pauses in speech **c)** to show a speaker trailed off **d)** to show words are missed out **e)** to show a pause in the action

Question 3 Answers may vary. Award 2 marks if all unnecessary information is removed and 1 mark for a good attempt. **a)** The house . . . could be dangerous . . . so it has to be demolished. **b)** Skate-parks . . . are being built in many residential areas . . . **c)** If you go swimming in a lake . . . wear a wet suit and always have someone . . . with you

Challenge Answers will vary.

Page 39 Parenthesis
Question 1

	Explain a word	Emphasise a point	Show what the writer is thinking	Add extra information
(though I don't think that is true)			✔	
– in other words, your skull –	✔			
, who was tall and thin,				✔
– and I mean really tall.		✔		
(a set of lines for writing music)	✔			
– what a stupid idea.			✔	
(its babies live in there for six weeks)				✔

Question 2 b), c) and **e)** ticked

Question 3 Answers may vary slightly. Sample answers: **a)** Tim always got his own way. He was spoilt. **b)** The paediatrician visited the ward. She is the children's doctor. **c)** The teacher was being unfair about the party. I thought he was really unfair. **d)** Some people do what I ask straight away. They are usually the intelligent ones.

Question 4 a) The Owls (who are based in Hillsborough, Sheffield) are a great football team. **b)** Tigers (with their excellent camouflage) are magnificent hunters. **c)** My favourite day (apart from my birthday) is the last day of term. **d)** Algebra (maths with letters) is lots of fun.

Challenge Answers will vary. Sample answer:
The party, which was in the village square, was enjoyed by everyone (even Mrs Pims – probably anyway). Gill – she's my best friend now – baked a cake. She called it a roulade (a cake made with meringue and cream) which was delicious – really delicious!

Page 41 comparatives and superlatives
Question 1

Adjective	Comparative	Superlative
thin	thinner	thinnest
tiny	tinier	tiniest
unfortunate	more unfortunate	most unfortunate
fit	fitter	fittest
little	littler	littlest
good	better	best
bad	worse	worst
self-conscious	more self-conscious	most self-conscious
fascinating	more fascinating	most fascinating
far	further	furthest

Question 2 a) bigger **b)** better **c)** largest **d)** prettier **e)** worst **f)** more sensible **g)** angriest **h)** best

Question 3 a) shorter **b)** taller **c)** Caitlin **d)** smallest, Barti

Challenge Answers will vary.

Page 43 Prefixes
Question 1 international, transnational mid-Atlantic, transatlantic semiconscious, hyperconscious interactive, hyperactive

Question 2 a) script; date; mortem; natal **b)** gone hand; thought; name **c)** lace; view; weave; marry **d)** rational; resolute; replaceable; religious

Question 3 Answers may vary. Sample answers: **a)** transaction, translate, transport, transform, transplant **b)** irregular, irrespective, irreproachable, irreversible, irreverent **c)** mid-air, midwinter, midsummer, midway, mid-week, midship **d)** interbreed, interchange, intergalactic, interplanetary, intercourse, interweave **e)** anti-aircraft, anti-personnel, anticlockwise, antidote, anticlimax

Question 4 a) transformed **b)** irresistible

Question 5 Answers will vary slightly. Sample answers: **a)** prevent freezing **b)** before midday **c)** a larger than normal supermarket **d)** half joined **e)** the land in the middle **f)** not responsible **g)** somebody that stars with someone else **h)** after the war

Challenge Examples may vary. Sample answers:

ante–	before	ante-room, antecedent
counter–	opposite, opposition	counteract, counter-attack, counter-clockwise
under–	below	underarm, undercarriage, undersecretary, underwear
auto–	self	automatic, autobiography, autopilot
mal–	bad / ly	malnutrition, malpractice
mono–	one, single	monorail, monocle, monotony

Page 45 Suffixes
Question 1 a) satisfy **b)** art **c)** gang **d)** friend **e)** adventure **f)** god

Question 2 a) child; new; fool; sweet **b)** collect; decorate; rotate; direct **c)** dental; piano; chemistry; science **d)** great; sick; sweet; thick

Question 3 Answers will vary. Sample answers: **a)** collision, decision, revision **b)** conscious, delicious, ridiculous **c)** advertise, harmonise, trivialise **d)** demonic, realistic, characteristic **e)** murderess, stewardess, waitress

Question 4 a) realistic **b)** privacy **c)** collision

Question 5 Answers will vary slightly. Sample answers: **a)** a person who plays the cello **b)** something that has style **c)** in the state of rotating **d)** in the process of being forgiven **e)** show on / make for television **f)** a female prince / daughter of a king and queen

Challenge Answers will vary.

Page 47 Plurals
Question 1 a) ditches **b)** hoaxes **c)** lorries **d)** leaves **e)** counters **f)** pianos **g)** gases **h)** potatoes

Question 2 a) men **b)** feet **c)** people **d)** appendices (accept appendixes) **e)** mice **f)** these **g)** oxen **h)** fungi (allow funguses)

Question 3 moose; spaghetti; headquarters; tuna; bison

Question 4 Answers will vary. Sample answers: **a)** We stopped at the crossroads. All the crossroads were blocked off. **b)** The sheep was big. The sheep were frightened. **c)** The piece of furniture was delivered. We put the bedroom furniture into the hall.

d) Westies are a species of dog. Every species is part of a classification group.

Challenge Answers will vary. Sample answers: deer / deer; moose / moose; salmon / salmon; stigma / stigmatai; louse /lice; goose / geese

Page 49 Homophones and similar words

Question 1 Answers will vary but check that these meanings are conveyed: **a)** affect (verb), to affect the outcome; effect (noun) the result or outcome or (verb) to effect so that it makes or brings about **b)** aloud, out loud; allowed, permitted **c)** farther, a distance away; father, a male parent **d)** altar, a religious table; alter, change **e)** compliment, to make nice remarks; complement, to make something complete or better **f)** profit, money gained; prophet, someone who foretells the future **g)** whose, possessive pronoun (shows something belongs to someone); who's, contraction of 'who is' or 'who has' **h)** advice, (noun) a piece of advice; advise, to recommend what someone should do **i)** past (noun / adjective) referring to time or (preposition adverb) showing direction or place; passed, past tense of 'to pass' **j)** cereal, made from grain; serial, things that happen one after the other **k)** principal, the most important or the person in charge; principle, a truth or belief

Challenge Answers will vary. Sample answers: knight (a Medieval soldier) / night (after the sun has gone down); mail (what is received in the post) / male (a man); flea (an insect) / flee (run away); meat (food from an animal) / meet (get together) medal (a prize for winning) / meddle (interfere); sweet (pudding)/ suite (set of).

Page 51 Synonyms and antonyms

Question 1 a) terminate **b)** commission **c)** determined **d)** abundance **e)** atrocious

Question 2 a) confident, wary **b)** envious, content **c)** failure, triumph

Question 3 a) buy, sell **b)** entrance, exit

Question 4 Sentence answers will vary. The correct antonyms are: **a)** export / import **b)** departure / arrival **c)** overweight / underweight **d)** interior / exterior **e)** victory / defeat **f)** insult / compliment

Challenge Answers will vary. Sample answer: suffocation / asphyxiation

Page 53 Concision

Question 1 A

a) prophet —— person who tells what is in the future

b) bridle — reason why something must not be done

c) villain — harness that goes on a horse's head to help you guide it

d) objection — person who is wicked

Question 1B Answers will vary. Check the sentences make sense. Sample answers: **a)** The prophet said it would be a new beginning. **b)** I put the bridle on before I rode the horse. **c)** The villain broke into Dad's garage. **d)** Sara made an objection to doing her homework when she should be playing.

Question 2

| c | pension | a | ventilate | f | excavate |
| d | blemish | e | terminate | b | guarantee |

Question 3 a) dilapidated **b)** coax **c)** simile **d)** extricate **e)** incinerate

Challenge Answers will vary.

Page 55 Etymology

Question 1

Word	Etymology
alarm	Chinese – *ke-tsiap* was a sauce they invented at the end of the 17th century.
ketchup	Italian – means 'To arms!'
robot	French – means good air. In the Middle Ages if you smelled good you were thought to be healthier and happier.
bungalow	Old German – *hus* means 'house' and *bunda* means 'owner'. A homeowner would be a good person to marry!
debonair	Hindi – means 'one-storey house'.
husband	Latin – *liber* means 'to peel' and would refer to the inner bark of a tree that manuscripts were written on.
library	Italian – small ball or pebble that was used to cast a vote in a box.
ballot	Czech – means 'worker'.
salary	Rome – soldiers were paid a handful of salt a day, which was replaced by money as it was easier to transport, so soldiers' got their salt money (*salarium*).
sinister	Old English – stol for 'throne'.
stool	Mediaeval French – means 'cooked twice'.
biscuit	Latin for left; the left side was thought to be evil.

Question 2 Answers will vary. Sample answers:

Examples
aquamarine, aquarium, aqueduct, aquifer, aquadrome
automobile, autonomy, autograph, automatic
globe, global, globule, globous, globular
microscope, microphone, micro-organism

Question 3

Meaning
alone
death
life

Challenge Answers will vary. Sample answers: Latin, Greek, Spanish, Italian, French, German.

Page 57 Idioms

Question 1 Answers will vary. Sample answers: **a)** lend a hand – help out **b)** raining cats and dogs – raining heavily **c)** jump to it – hurry up **d)** cost an arm and a leg – very expensive **e)** racing against the clock – hurrying

Question 2 Answers will vary. Sample answers: **a)** She was wearing designer clothes that were right over the top! **b)** He was making such a noise I told him to pipe down. **c)** Tongue in cheek he said, "Let's go skating at midnight." **d)** After breaking the picture Jerry broke the lamp, which was the last straw

Question 3 Blood is thicker than water.

Challenge Answers will vary. Sample answers: up and running; beat about the bush; catch one's eye; couch potato; get on one's nerves; in over one's head; in the red; pull someone's leg; sleep on it; wet behind the ears

Page 59 Figurative language

Question 1

as high as a kite — simile
the car screamed — metaphor
the girl mumbled — personification
onomatopoeia
the fog was a grey blanket   the crisps crunched   flew like a bird

Question 2 Answers will vary. Standard similes are given here: **a)** a giraffe **b)** a ghost / sheet **c)** an owl / Solomon **d)** a bear / wolf **e)** a lion **f)** a peacock **g)** a post **h)** a bat **i)** a bee **j)** an eel

Question 3 a) tick tock **b)** smash **c)** buzz **d)** click **e)** sizzle **f)** quack

Question 4 Answers will vary. Sample answers:

The bus	was as slow as a snail.
	was a people-eating monster.
	grumbled all the way up the hill.
	crashed.
The flowers	were as white as snow.
	were stars scattered on the grass.
	waved as we walked past.
	whispered.
The wind	was as fierce as a tiger.
	was a roaring, fighting beast.
	whistled happily as it danced around the chimney.
	whooshed.

Challenge Answers will vary, but should refer to the picture or effect the author was trying to create. (Do not accept general answers such as, "for emphasis" or "to show what it was like".)

Now try these questions:

1 Join these sentences using a semi-colon.

a) Cars are a major problem. Parking cars can be an even bigger problem.

_____

(1 mark each)

/4

b) The book was interesting. The film was really boring.

_____

c) Eleanor could run for hours. Isobel preferred to ride her bike.

_____

d) It was hot in the valley. Up in the hills it was cool.

_____

2 Match the parts of the sentence halves.

The maths test was easy;	Carol was the worst.
Joshua was the best player;	Nye liked vegetables.
Andy was very cross;	the reading test was hard.
George liked meat;	Mr Lomas wasn't bothered.
Azim enjoyed reading;	Lekh enjoyed making models.

(1 mark each)

/5

3 Choose the best ending for this sentence:

Jake laughed till he cried;

a) Susan cooked the tea. b) because it was funny. c) Tom just cried.

(1 mark)

/1

4 Complete these sentences, making sure that there is a complete sentence after the semi-colon.

a) Beth liked going shopping; _____

b) Zak went to bed early; _____

c) The dragon flew gracefully over the lake; _____

d) Exercise helps to keep you healthy; _____

(1 mark for each line)

/4

5 Write the first part of these sentences. Make sure there is a complete sentence before the semi-colon.

a) _____ ; Caitlin spent the evening reading.

b) _____ ; Billy mended the model.

c) _____ ; Barti wanted to go to the seaside.

d) _____ ; Gill could play the piano.

(1 mark for each line)

/4

CHALLENGE Find out about other conditions for using a semi-colon and write some examples to illustrate your findings.

31

Colons

Using colons correctly is easy if you learn a couple of simple rules.

Use after a full sentence before a list.

> I had to pack a lot for the trip: a whistle, a first aid kit, my lunch and spare clothes.

Use to separate two sentences where the second sentence explains the first sentence.

> The book was informative: it told him everything he needed to know about motors.

For both of these uses the colon needs to be preceded by a full sentence.

Let's practise!

Match the first half of the sentence to the most appropriate second half

Isidore enjoyed his lunch:	Max was talking very loudly.
	he liked playing football.
	pasta and chicken were his favourite foods.

1 Read the question, then read it again. What are you being asked to do?

Choose the best ending to the sentence.

2 Think what the first part of the sentence says.

It tells us about Isidore's lunch.

3 Think why there is a colon at the end of it.

Colons introduce a list or another sentence that illustrates or explains the first sentence.

4 Check the options for the second part of the sentence.

There aren't any lists so there must be a sentence that explains or illustrates the first part of the sentence.

5 What are the second sentences about?

The first is about Max talking. The next is about playing football. The last is about what food he liked.

6 Decide which matches most closely with the first sentence.

The one about food matches to the sentence about lunch.

7 Write the two sentences, separating them with a colon.

Isidore enjoyed his lunch: pasta and chicken were his favourite foods.

Now try these questions:

1 Amend these sentences using a colon to join them together.
  a) The children didn't finish their work. They had spent too much time talking.
  b) The box was heavy. It was full of old books.
  c) Cydney was worried. She hadn't seen Charlie for two days.
  d) There was a loud bang. The wall collapsed.

(1 mark for each line)

/4

2 Match the parts of the sentence halves.

Andy was a good coach:	he had studied every night.
Joshua was the best player:	he spent an hour on it every night.
Max wanted to pass the exam:	he went to the library every week.
George liked his computer:	he made Lori train properly.
Azim enjoyed reading:	he was the team captain.

(1 mark each)

/5

3 Write appropriate lists after the colons in these sentences:
  a) Lani bought lots at the shops: _____
  b) Eleanor had lots of animals on the farm: _____
  c) Robert went on lots of rides at the fair: _____
  d) Joe invited his friends to tea: _____

(1 mark for each line)

/4

4 Complete these sentences, making sure that there is a complete sentence after the colon.
  a) Indi had the best party ever: _____
  b) Javinder had a busy weekend: _____
  c) William knew what he had to do: _____
  d) Sharks can be dangerous animals: _____

(1 mark for each line)

/4

5 Write the first part of these sentences. Make sure there is a complete sentence before the colon.
  a) _____ : fish chips, peas and ice cream.
  b) _____ : red, yellow, blue and green.
  c) _____ : Nye, Jake, Rowan and Barti.
  d) _____ : Monday, Tuesday and Thursday.

(1 mark for each line)

/4

 **CHALLENGE** Find out about other ways a colon can be used and write some examples.

Hyphens

Definition: Hyphens are short dashes between two words.
For example, forget-me-not.

Hyphens are used for	Examples
some compound nouns	mother-in-law, hang-glider
verbs made from two nouns	to ice-skate, to court-martial
compound adjectives	green-fingered, long-eared
adding a prefix to some words	ex-wife, re-examine
clarity, to distinguish words	re-sign / resign, re-creation / recreation
writing fractions and numbers less than 100 as words	one-sixth, forty-six

Let's practise!

Match these compound words with their meanings.

green-fingered	not being open to new ideas
long-eared	easy going
happy-go-lucky	smart
well-dressed	good at growing things
narrow-minded	having long ears

1 Read the question, then read it again. What are you being asked to do?

> **Match the words to their meanings.**

2 Look for any words that you are confident you know.

> Long-eared **must mean** having long ears. Well-dressed **must mean** smart.

3 Check the words and meanings that are left.

> green-fingered   **easy going**
> happy-go-lucky   **good at growing things**
> narrow-minded   **not being open to new ideas**

4 Select the most appropriate meanings.

> **Green-fingered** sounds like it is to do with growing things. **Happy-go-lucky** sounds like easy going, **which leaves** narrow-minded **as not being open to new ideas.**

5 Join the words to their meanings.

> green-fingered — not being open to new ideas
> long-eared — easy going
> happy-go-lucky — smart
> well-dressed — good at growing things
> narrow-minded — having long ears

Now try these questions:

1 Underline the compound adjective in these sentences.
a) Joe has always been accident-prone.
b) The computer-aided research was very expensive.
c) Mr Kwec was a good-looking man.
d) The juice was supposed to be sugar-free.
e) The power-driven teacher wanted to be a head-teacher.

(1 mark each)

/5

2 Match these compound words to their meaning.

custom-built	ready to be filmed
ex-husband	man that someone used to be married to
camera-ready	built to the customer's specification
self-pity	feeling sorrow for yourself
mayor-elect	everything paid for
all-inclusive	the person selected to be the next mayor

(1 mark each)

/6

3 Write a sentence for each of these compound words.
a) quick-thinking _____
_____
b) bad-tempered _____
_____
c) muddle-headed _____
_____
d) co-owner _____
_____
e) seventy-six _____
_____

(1 mark each)

/5

4 Write these numbers correctly as words
a) 55 _____ b) 71 _____
c) $^2/_3$ _____ d) 98 _____
e) 27 _____ f) 43 _____

(1 mark each)

/6

CHALLENGE

Find some hyphenated words in a reading book.
Write them down and explain what they mean.

35

Ellipsis

Definition: An ellipsis is a set of three dots …

Use ellipsis marks in formal writing when a word or words are missed out of a quote:

> The mayor said, "Our schools give the best education …"

Use ellipsis marks in informal writing to show a character trailing off in a speech:

> "Perhaps they won't mind …" stammered Alex.

a pause for emphasis or thought

> She looked … she waited … she crossed.

Let's practise!

Use an ellipsis to shorten this quote so that just the main message is written:

> The head-teacher, in assembly, said, "After careful thought, having considered the problem from every angle, I have come to a decision. Because there are too many children to fit into the hall, I have decided that there will be two sittings at lunch time, with the younger children eating first, and then the older children going in after that. I hope you all understand why that is necessary."

1 Read the question, then read it again. What are you being asked to do?

Give the important message from the quote.

2 Underline the important information.

<u>The head-teacher,</u> in assembly, said, "After careful thought, having considered the problem from every angle, <u>I have come to a decision.</u> Because there are too many children to fit into the hall, <u>I have decided that there will be two sittings at lunch time,</u> with the younger children eating first, and then the older children going in after that. I hope you all understand why that is necessary."

3 Write the important information, putting an ellipsis where words are missed out.

The head-teacher … said, "I have come to a decision … I have decided that there will be two sittings at lunch time …"

TOP TIP Don't overuse the ellipsis. It loses its impact if there are too many in your writing.

TOP TIP

Now try these questions:

1 Complete the table to show why an ellipsis has been used.

	Words missed out	A speaker trailed off	To show a pause
The fireman said, " ... it was started deliberately."			
"I'm not sure ..." whispered Caitlin.			
Ofsted reported that the children ... behaved well.			
Rowan waited ... and waited ... and waited.			
"Please ... stop it ... don't ..." shouted Charlotte.			
"I wonder ..." said Mrs Butcher.			

(1 mark each)

/6

2 Explain why an ellipsis has been used in these sentences.
a) The police report stated that the man ... was dangerous.

_____

b) "Steer to the left ... no, to the right ... no to the left!" called Callum.

_____

c) "If you did that ..." said Ms Moore, thoughtfully.

_____

d) In court the verdict ... was guilty.

_____

e) They saw the fox ... the fox saw them.

_____

(1 mark each)

/5

3 Write the important messages from these quotes, using an ellipsis to show where words are missed out.
a) The house, which has been left empty for years and years, is falling apart. It could be dangerous if people tried to go inside so it has to be demolished.

_____

b) If you go swimming in a lake, which can be very dangerous, especially if the water is cold, you need to take precautions: wear a wet suit which is suitable for swimming activities and always have someone on the bank or with you in the water in case you get into difficulties.

_____

(2 marks for each line)

/4

CHALLENGE Look through books in the library and write down any uses of the ellipsis you find. Keep a note of books where a lot of ellipses are used. What type of books are they?

Parenthesis

Definition: A parenthesis is an extra word or phrase that is put into a sentence. It can be used to:

- show what someone is thinking
- add extra information for the reader
- explain the meaning of a word
- emphasise a point.

Parentheses are usually written in brackets, between commas or between dashes.

Examples:

a) Adam (who is rather strange) collects plastic bottles.
b) Adam – who is rather strange – collects plastic bottles.
c) Adam, who is rather strange, collects plastic bottles.

Let's practise!

Remove the brackets from this sentence and write the same information in two sentences.

The Statue of Liberty (standing in the harbour at New York) was a symbol of hope to all immigrants to America.

1	Read the question, then read it again. What are you being asked to do?	**Remove the brackets and put information into two sentences**
2	Write the sentence given without the information in parenthesis.	The Statue of Liberty was a symbol of hope to all immigrants to America.
3	Read the information that was in parenthesis.	(standing in the harbour at New York)
4	Make it into a complete sentence.	The Statue of Liberty stands in the harbour in New York.
5	Read the sentences together – do you need to change any words?	The Statue of Liberty is used in both sentences so we could replace it in one with a pronoun.
6	Decide on an order for the sentences and write your final answer.	The Statue of Liberty stands in the harbour in New York. It was a symbol of hope to all immigrants to America.

TOP TIP

- If your sentence contains hyphens, avoid using dashes as they look very similar. Use brackets or commas instead.
- If your sentence already contains commas, avoid using commas as it will get rather confusing to read! Use brackets or dashes instead.

TOP TIP

Now try these questions:

1 Complete the table to show the function of the comments in parenthesis:

	Explain a word	Emphasise a point	Show what the writer is thinking	Add extra information
(though I don't think that is true)				
– in other words, your skull –				
, who was tall and thin,				
– and I mean really tall.				
(a set of lines for writing music)				
– what a stupid idea.				
(its babies live in there for six weeks)				

(1 mark each)

/7

2 Tick the sentences where the parenthesis is correctly used.
a) Jack and Kerry always (went to) town.
b) The fermata (or pause sign) is frequently used in music.
c) My dad is fantastic at cooking (or so he thinks).
d) The car which was new (had cost a lot of money).
e) Imran (being a natural at art) always got to help with the stage backdrop.

(1 mark for each line)

/5

3 Remove the brackets from these sentences and write the same information in two sentences each time.
a) Tim (who was spoilt) always got his own way.

_____

b) The paediatrician (children's doctor) visited the ward.

_____

c) The teacher was being unfair (and I mean really unfair) about the party.

_____

d) Some people (usually the intelligent ones) do what I ask straight away.

_____

(1 mark for each line)

/4

4 Add the missing brackets in these sentences.
a) The Owls who are based in Hillsborough, Sheffield are a great football team.
b) Tigers with their excellent camouflage are magnificent hunters.
c) My favourite day apart from my birthday is the end of term.
d) Algebra maths with letters is lots of fun.

(1 mark each)

/5

 **CHALLENGE** Write a description of a party using different types of parenthesis in your writing.

Comparatives and superlatives

Definitions: The comparative compares two things and usually ends in –er or uses the word more.

The superlative compares more than two things and usually ends in –est or uses the word most.

a) The red car is faster than the blue, but the blue car is more comfortable.

b) This school is the greatest school in the world!

c) It is the most expensive camera I've ever used.

Some rules for forming comparatives and superlatives:

small	smaller	smallest	Simple adjectives, add –er for the comparative and –est for the superlative
high	higher	highest	
fast	faster	fastest	
wise	wiser	wisest	Adjectives that end in –e, add –r for the comparison and –st for the superlative
late	later	latest	
brave	braver	bravest	
hot	hotter	hottest	Adjectives with a vowel and single consonant, double the consonant and add –er for the comparative and –est for the superlative
wet	wetter	wettest	
sad	sadder	saddest	
pretty	prettier	prettiest	Adjectives that end in –y, change the y to i and add –er for the comparative and –est for the superlative
happy	happier	happiest	
friendly	friendlier	friendliest	
intelligent	more intelligent	most intelligent	Most words with two or more syllables use more to make the comparative and most to make the superlative
peaceful	more peaceful	most peaceful	
talkative	more talkative	most talkative	

TOP TIP

TOP TIP

Some two-syllable words can use –er and –est or more and most.
For example:
simpler – more simple   friendliest – most friendly   hungrier – more hungry   angriest – most angry

Now try these questions:

1 Complete the table, forming each word correctly.

Adjective	Comparative	Superlative
	thinner	
		tiniest
unfortunate		
fit		
little		
	better	
		worst
		most self-conscious
	more fascinating	
		furthest

(1 mark for each line)

/10

2 Write the adjectives in brackets on the line in the correct form.

a) London is (big)_____than Manchester.

b) Imran is (good)_____ at writing than he was last year.

c) The (large) _____ mammal in the world is the blue whale.

d) Holly gets (pretty) _____ every year.

e) Mark is the (bad)_____ listener in the school!

f) Bob has a (sensible) _____ attitude than Max.

g) Ms Kahn is the (angry)_____I've ever seen her.

h) Charlie is the (good)_____singer in the choir.

(1 mark each)

/8

3 Read this passage.

Tom is the smallest child in Year 5. Libby is taller than Lucy Mae but smaller than William. Caitlin is taller than Joshua, who is taller than William. Barti is shorter than Lucy Mae.

Now choose the correct word to complete each sentence.

a) Tom is (shorter / taller) than William.

b) William is (shorter / taller) than Lucy Mae.

c) The tallest child is (Lucy Mae / Libby / Joshua / William / Barti / Caitlin).

d) The next (smaller / small / smallest) after Tom is (Barti / Lucy Mae / Libby).

(1 mark each)

/4

 Devise a quiz for your friends to check they know how to form different comparatives and superlatives.

Prefixes

Definition: A prefix is a group of letters placed at the start of a word.
The prefix changes the meaning of the word.
Knowing prefixes can make spelling easier and increase your vocabulary.

Purpose: Some common prefixes with their meanings are:

Prefix	Meaning	Examples
anti– ant–	against / opposite to	antibiotic, Antarctic,
fore–	before	forefinger, foreshadow
inter–	between	interact, interface
post–	after	postpone, postnatal
co–	together	coeducation, coordinate
il–	not	illegal, illiberal
ir–	not	irrelevant, irredeemable
mid–	in the middle of	midterm, midnight
semi–	half	semiconscious, semicircle
hyper–	more than normal	hypersonic, hyperbole
trans–	across	translate, transnational

Let's practise!
Use your knowledge of prefixes to write the meaning of these words.

hypercritical	semi-precious

1 Read the question, then read it again. What are you being asked to do?

Work out the meaning of the words.

2 Look at the first word and think what the prefix means.

hypercritical – hyper– **means more than normal.**

3 Use this to give the meaning of the word.

hypercritical **means more critical than is normal.**

4 Look at the second word and think what the prefix means.

semi-precious – semi– **means half**

5 Use this to give the meaning of the word.

semi-precious **means half precious so that is valuable but not really expensive.**

Now try these questions:

1 Use prefixes from the table on the previous page with each of these words to make two different words.

(1 mark each)

/8

_____ national   _____ Atlantic _____ conscious _____ active

_____ national   _____ Atlantic _____ conscious _____ active

2 Circle the four words that would go with these prefixes.

a) post–   script date mortem reason natal figure

b) fore–   ward gone hundred hand thought list name

c) inter– lace sense stop view weave live marry

d) ir–   rational racial resolute reduce replaceable religious react

(1 mark each)

/16

3 Think of three new words that start with each of these prefixes. Don't use the examples already given in the table on the previous page!

a) trans– _____ _____ _____

b) ir–   _____ _____ _____

c) mid–   _____ _____ _____

d) inter–   _____ _____ _____

e) anti–   _____ _____ _____

(3 marks each)

/15

4 Put the correct word on the line to complete each sentence.

a) The decorators _____ the old house into a modern habitation.

(transformed informed reformed disformed uniformed)

b) Andy thought the cakes were _____.

(resistable irrespective irresistible unresistible inresistible)

(1 mark each)

/2

5 Use your knowledge of prefixes to explain these words.

a) antifreeze   _____

b) forenoon   _____

c) hypermarket   _____

d) semi-detached   _____

e) midland   _____

f) irresponsible   _____

g) co-star   _____

h) post-war   _____

(1 mark each)

/8

CHALLENGE Make a prefix table using these prefixes:

ante– counter– under– aut(o)– mal– mon(o)–

Suffixes

Definition: A suffix is a group of letters placed at the end of a word. The suffix changes the meaning of the word.

Knowing suffixes can make spelling easier and increase your vocabulary.

Beware – some suffixes change the spelling of the word!

Examples:

Suffix	Makes	Meaning	Example
–acy	noun	state of being	piracy
–ist		one who does	pianist
–dom		place or state	kingdom
–ess		female	actress
–tion / –sion		state of being	extension
–ster		person	mobster
–ness		state of being	friendliness
–ize / –ise	verb	to make or become	liquidise
–ish	adjective	have the quality of	foolish
–ic / –ac		like / pertaining to	aquatic
–ous		having / full of	delicious

Let's practise!

Match the suffixes and the words to make the words mean the state of being. Change the word spelling if necessary.

Suffixes:	–acy	–dom	–tion	–sion	–ness
Words:	diplomat	elated	sad	free	

1 Read the question, then read it again. What are you being asked to do?

Make the words mean a state of being.

2 Look at the first word and think of it as a state of being.

diplomat – you would be in a state of diplomacy.

3 Look at the next word.

elated – you would be full of elation.

4 Look at the next word.

sad – you would be full of sadness.

5 Look at the last word.

free – you would be in a state of freedom.

TOP TIP
When you learn suffixes, their spellings and meanings, link them to learning the etymology (origin) of words. Since lots of words use the same suffixes, you learn new words and spellings in one go.
TOP TIP

Now try these questions:

1 Remove the suffix and write the root word correctly.

a) satisfaction _____ b) artist _____ c) gangster _____

d) friendship _____ e) adventurous _____ f) goddess _____

(1 mark each)

/6

2 Circle the four words that would go with the suffix to make new words.

a) –ish   child   new   cost   fool   sweet

b) –tion   collect   decorate   rotate   direct   fate

c) –ist   dental   piano   record   chemistry   science

d) –ness   great   sick   sweet   think   thick

(4 marks for each line)

/16

3 Think of three different words that end with each of these suffixes.

a) –sion   _____   _____   _____

b) –ous   _____   _____   _____

c) –ise   _____   _____   _____

d) –ic   _____   _____   _____

e) –ess   _____   _____   _____

(3 marks for each line)

/15

4 Put the missing word on the line to complete each sentence correctly.

a) The model looked very _____ .
   (realicist / realistic / realist / realic)

b) Her _____ is important to the Queen.
   (private / privately / privacy / privateness)

c) The _____ on the motorway caused a lot of damage.
   (collision / collition / colliding / collidiment)

(1 mark for each line)

/3

5 Write the meaning of each word.

a) cellist   _____

b) stylish   _____

c) rotation   _____

d) forgiveness   _____

e) televise   _____

f) princess   _____

(1 mark for each line)

/6

CHALLENGE Find as many suffixes as you can on one page of a reading book and then research their meanings.

Plurals

A quick revision! **Irregular plurals:**

Ending in	To the form the plural	Example	Exceptions
ch, x, s, sh	add –es	watches	
o	add –es	volcanoes	words of Spanish and Italian origin, e.g. tacos
y	drop the y and add –ies	cities	words ending in –ey, e.g. donkeys
is	change the i to e	crises	
us	drop the us and add i	stimuli	
f	drop the f and add ves	loaves	e.g. chefs, beliefs

Other irregular plurals: These do not follow the usual patterns. Examples:

child – children   person – people   man – men   woman – women
ox – oxen   foot – feet   goose – geese   mouse – mice   tooth – teeth

Zero plurals: These plurals are exactly the same as the singular noun. Examples:

aircraft   fish   headquarters   sheep   species
deer   moose   crossroads   salmon   barracks   pike

Let's practise!
Use aircraft in a sentence that shows it is singular and then in a different sentence that shows it is plural

(1) 1Read the question, then read it again. What are you being asked to do?

Write two sentences, one showing aircraft as a singular noun and one showing it as a plural.

(2) Think about the singular.

That means there is one aircraft.

(3) Write a sentence about one aircraft.

The aircraft is approaching the runway.

(4) Think about the plural.

That means there are two or more aircraft.

(5) Write a sentence about more than one aircraft.

The aircraft were circling above the airport, queuing for the landing strip.

(6) Write your answers.

The aircraft is approaching the runway. The aircraft were circling above the airport, queuing for the landing strip.

Now try these questions:

1 Write the plural of these nouns.

    a) ditch   _____

    b) hoax   _____

    c) lorry   _____

    d) leaf   _____

    e) counter   _____

    f) piano   _____

    g) gas   _____

    h) potato   _____

(1 mark each)

/8

2 Write the plural of these irregular nouns.

    a) man   _____

    b) foot   _____

    c) person   _____

    d) appendix   _____

    e) mouse   _____

    f) this   _____

    g) ox   _____

    h) fungus   _____

(1 mark each)

/8

3 Circle the nouns which are zero plurals.

tadpole	fleece	moose	jubilee	spaghetti	headquarters
office	cooker	tuna	carpet	network	bison

(1 mark for each correct one)

/5

4 Use these zero plurals in two sentences each. In one sentence use them as a singular noun and in the other as a plural noun.

    a) crossroads _____

    _____

    _____

    _____

    b) sheep _____

    _____

    _____

    _____

(1 mark for each sentence)

/8

    c) furniture _____

    _____

    _____

    _____

    d) species _____

    _____

    _____

    _____

CHALLENGE Use the Internet and dictionaries to list all the irregular and zero plurals you can find.

Homophones and similar words

Some words are often used incorrectly, even by adults. Learn how to use them and you are getting ahead of the game!

> **Similar words that end in ce and se:**
> advice / advise   device / devise   practice / practise   licence / license

> **The words ending in ce are nouns**
> (imagine changing the c to an a and then you know it is **a thing**):
> a piece of advice   a practice   a device   a licence

> **The words ending in se are verbs.**
> (imagine the s as a wriggly letter and you know it is doing something)
> to advise   to devise   to practise   to license

Let's practise!

Put the words prophesy and prophecy in the correct places in this sentence.

When the man started to _____ , he made a _____ that affected everyone.

1	Read the question, then read it again. What are you being asked to do?	**Put the words correctly in the sentence.**
2	Think what type of word is needed in the first space.	**started to _____ He was doing something so we need a verb.**
3	Check which of the words is a verb.	**The word with s is the verb (it's a wriggly letter!) so he started to prophesy.**
4	Think what type of word is needed in the second space.	**made a _____ He made something so we need a noun.**
5	Check which of the words is a noun.	**The word with c is the noun (make the c to a) so he made a prophecy.**
6	Write the complete sentence.	**When the man started to prophesy, he made a prophecy that affected everyone.**

TOP TIP **TOP TIP**

Use these clues to remember these words
stationary – not moving (think of not getting away from point a)
stationery – papers, envelopes, etc. (e for envelopes and easy to write)

48

Now try these questions:

1 Use these words in sentences to illustrate their meaning. Check in a dictionary first if you need to.

a) affect _____

    effect _____

b) aloud _____

    allowed _____

c) farther _____

    father _____

d) altar _____

    alter _____

e) compliment _____

    complement _____

(1 mark for each pair)

f) profit _____

    prophet _____

/11

g) whose _____

    who's _____

h) advice _____

    advise _____

i) past _____

    passed _____

j) cereal _____

    serial _____

k) principal _____

    principle _____

CHALLENGE

Find other pairs of words that are commonly used incorrectly and write them with their definitions.

Synonyms and antonyms

Definitions: Synonyms are words that have the same (or a similar) meaning.

Antonyms are words that have opposite meanings.

Finding synonyms and antonyms is not only fun, it also increases your vocabulary.

Examples:

Word	Synonym	Antonym
wisdom	intelligence	foolishness
endure	withstand	capitulate
solemn	serious	joyous
reveal	uncover	conceal
frail	weak	robust
hopeful	optimistic	hopeless
natural	genuine	artificial
hindrance	impediment	help

Let's practise!

Fill the blanks in this sentence with a pair of antonyms.

> **It took 80 years to _____ the cathedral and a few minutes to _____ it.**

(1) Read the question, then read it again. What are you being asked to do?

Find a pair of antonyms that will complete the sentence.

(2) Think about what information the sentence contains.

It tells you that something took a long time and the opposite happened very quickly.

(3) Consider an antonym pair that might fit.

Find / lose – no, if it took 80 years to find the cathedral how could you lose it? Build – it could take 80 years to build a cathedral. The antonym of build is demolish. You could demolish a cathedral in minutes if you blew it up.

(4) Write the complete sentence.

It took 80 years to build the cathedral and a few minutes to demolish it.

TOP TIP Learning new words and their meanings helps to build an effective, rich vocabulary. The more you know, the better you can communicate. Look up synonym and antonym games on the Internet to help you learn more quickly. **TOP TIP**

Now try these questions:

1 Underline the odd word out in each list of synonyms.
a) terminate, commence, start, originate
b) sympathy, compassion, commission, care
c) lenient, tolerant, easygoing, determined
d) wilt, wither, abundance, shrivel
e) fantastic, atrocious, marvellous, brilliant

(1 mark each)

/5

2 Highlight a synonym and underline an antonym for each word.
a) cautious   confident   conscious   wary   weary
b) jealous   extensive   envious   content   contentious
c) success   failure   uncertainty   triumph   abrupt

(1 mark for each line)

/3

3 Write a pair of antonyms to complete each sentence.
a) We will have to _____ more flour if we want to make more cakes to _____ .
b) We came in through the main _____ and left through the fire _____ .

(1 mark for each line)

/2

4 Write the antonyms of these words and then write a sentence containing both words.
a) export   _____

_____

b) departure   _____

_____

c) overweight   _____

_____

d) interior   _____

_____

e) victory   _____

_____

f) insult   _____

_____

(2 marks each)

/12

CHALLENGE   Use a thesaurus to find some words with at least four syllables, and write a synonym for each.

Concision

One way to achieve a higher level in English is to be able to say everything you want to say in as few words as possible. This is called concision. You need a large vocabulary to help you do this. The more words you know, the more have to choose from.

Let's practise!
Choose the word that best completes this sentence:

The twins were so _____, no one realised they were sisters.
(familiar   inconsiderate   dissimilar   impudent)

(1)	Read the question, then read it again. What are you being asked to do?	**Choose the best word to complete the sentence.**
(2)	Think about what the sentence says.	**It tells us that no one realised that the twins were sisters – we are looking for a reason.**
(3)	Consider the first available word.	**familiar** – that means friendly or well-known. That wouldn't stop people realising they were sisters.
(4)	Consider the second available word.	**inconsiderate** – that means thoughtless. If the twins were thoughtless that wouldn't stop people realising they were sisters.
(5)	Consider the third available word.	**dissimilar** – that means not alike. If the twins were not alike that might stop people realising they were sisters.
(6)	Check the final word.	**impudent** – that means cheeky. That wouldn't stop people realising they were sisters.
(7)	Write the best word on the line.	**The twins were so dissimilar, no one realised they were sisters.**

TOP TIP If you don't know any of the words, use a dictionary to find out what they mean. If you learn one new word every day, that would be over 300 new words by this time next year! **TOP TIP**

52

Now try these questions:

1 **A)** Match the word to the group of words it could replace.

a) prophet   person who tells what is in the future

b) bridle   reason why something must not be done

c) villain   goes on a horse's head to help you guide it

d) objection   person who is wicked

(1 mark each)

/4

B) Use each of the words correctly in a sentence.

a) (prophet) _____

b) (bridle) _____

c) (villain) _____

d) (objection) _____

(1 mark each)

/4

2 Choose the word from the box which could replace the underlined words in each sentence and write the letter of the sentence next to it.

	pension		ventilate		excavate
	blemish		terminate		guarantee

a) He opened the window to <u>let some fresh air into</u> the car.

b) The boy could <u>give an assurance that</u> the phone would work.

c) Rowan went to collect his <u>money that he received because he had retired.</u>

d) There was a <u>nasty, unpleasant mark</u> on the wall.

e) Olivia decided to <u>put an end to</u> the argument.

f) William was going to <u>dig out a large hole</u> where the house used to be.

(1 mark each)

/6

3 Circle the word that means:

a) worn out and needing repair

condemned   reclaimed   dilapidated   smouldered

b) persuade someone by encouragement

plead   coax   impartial   recommend

c) words used to compare something with something else

simile   metaphor   preposition   alliteration

d) to get free from

extensive   extinct   extinguish   extricate

e) to burn something to ashes

incidental   incisor   incinerate   incentive

(1 mark each)

/5

CHALLENGE   Use a dictionary and make a list of some words you don't already know with their meanings. Try to learn some of your new words.

Etymology

Definition: Etymology is the study of the origins of words. It looks at where words came from and how they have changed over time.

Etymology is fascinating and helps you to build and understand vocabulary. A good dictionary will tell you the origin of a word as well as its meaning today.

The words we use today have come from lots of different languages, although many of our words come from Greek and Latin.

Let's practise!

For each of these word roots, write two modern words that are related to the origin.

Word root	Origin	Meaning	Examples
mobilis	Latin	moveable	
astron	Greek	a star	

1	Read the question, then read it again. What are you being asked to do?	Find words that relate to the word root that is given.
2	Study the first word root.	*mobilis*, which means moveable, so we need words that look similar and are to do with moving.
3	Select words that are related.	mobile, mobility, immobile
4	Study the second word root.	*astron*, which means a star, so we need words that look similar and are to do with stars.
5	Select words that are related.	astronomy, astrology, astronaut
6	Complete the table.	

Word root	Origin	Meaning	Examples
mobilis	Latin	moveable	mobile, mobility, immobile
astron	Greek	a star	astronomy, astrology, astronaut

TOP TIP   Find a dictionary that tells you the etymology of words. Whenever you look up a word, check the etymology and use it to help you remember and understand the word.   **TOP TIP**

Now try these questions:

1 Match the word with its etymology.

Word	Etymology
alarm	Chinese – *ke-tsiap* was a sauce invented at the end of the 17th century.
ketchup	Italian – means 'To arms!'
robot	French – means 'good air'. In the Middle Ages if you smelled good you were thought to be healthier and happier.
bungalow	Old German – *hus* means 'house' and *bunda* means 'owner'. A homeowner would be a good person to marry!
debonair	Hindi – means 'one-storey house'.
husband	Latin – *liber* means 'to peel' and would refer to the inner bark of a tree that manuscripts were written on.
library	Italian – small ball or pebble that was used to cast a vote in a box.
ballot	Czech – means 'worker'.
salary	Rome – soldiers were paid a handful of salt a day, which was replaced by money as it was easier to transport, so soldiers got their salt money (*salarium*).
sinister	Old English – stol for 'throne'.
stool	Mediaeval French – means 'cooked twice'.
biscuit	Latin for left; the left side was thought to be evil.

(1 mark each)

/12

2 For each of these word roots, write two modern words that are related to the origin.

Word root	Origin	Meaning	Examples
aqua	Latin	water	
autos	Greek	self	
globus	Latin	sphere	
mikros	Greek	small	

(1 mark each)

/4

3 For each of these word roots, use the modern words to deduce (work out) the meaning of the root.

Word root	Origin	Meaning	Examples
solus	Latin		desolate, sole, solo, solipsism
mortis	Latin		mortal, mortuary, immortal, mortality
bios	Greek		biography, biology, biosphere, biologist

(1 mark each)

/3

CHALLENGE Use the Internet and an etymological dictionary to see how many languages you can find that have words we use or have adapted for the English language.

Idioms

Definition: Groups of words that do not mean exactly what they say!

Purpose: To convey meaning in a more colourful way.

Uses: In speech and informal writing.

Let's practise!

Underline the idiom and draw an arrow to the picture that shows what it means.

I'm feeling under the weather.

1 Read the question, then read it again. What are you being asked to do?

Find the idiom in the sentence and show what it means.

2 Look for the words in the sentence that you wouldn't really do or see.

I'm feeling – **that makes sense.**
under the weather – **how can you be under the weather?**

3 Underline those words.

under the weather.

4 Now think about or find out what the idiom means and join it to the correct meaning.

I'm feeling <u>under the weather.</u>

TOP TIP   Try to learn some new idioms – the more you know, the more chance you have to use them.   **TOP TIP**

TOP TIP   If people use idioms that you don't understand, ask them to explain them. That way you learn more! Here are two more idioms to learn:

Chew the fat
(means gossip
or idle chat)

Hit the sack
(means go
to bed)

TOP TIP

Now try these questions:

1 Underline the idioms in these sentences and explain what they mean.

a) If you lend a hand we can do it easily.

_____

b) It was raining cats and dogs.

_____

(1 mark each)

/5

c) We were told to jump to it.

_____

d) The tickets cost an arm and a leg.

_____

e) We were racing against the clock to beat the other team.

_____

2 Use these idioms to write sentences that show what they mean.
a) no room to swing a cat
   The house was so small there was no room to swing a cat!

b) over the top

_____

c) pipe down

(1 mark each)

/4

_____

d) tongue in cheek

_____

e) the last straw

_____

3 Find and write an idiom that means:

(1 mark)

the family bond is stronger than anything else

/1

_____

CHALLENGE Find and make a list of ten interesting idioms to use in your writing. You could try searching on the Internet.

Figurative language

Using figurative language makes your writing more expressive and interesting. It also extends your ability to use language to communicate.

Types of figurative language:

Simile	Onomatopoeia
This says something is like something else. The fire was as hot as the sun.	A word that makes the sound it describes. The paper rustled. 'Pop!' went the balloon. 
Metaphor	Personification
This says something is something else. The fire was the sun, blazing through the night. 	A special type of metaphor that gives an object human characteristics. The window winked at me. 

Let's practise!

Complete the sentence opening using each of the different types of figurative language shown.

The door	_____ (simile)
	_____ (metaphor)
	_____ (personification)
	_____ (onomatopoeia)

1 Read the question, then read it again. What are you being asked to do?

Use figurative language to put endings on the sentence.

2 Think of a simile. Use the words as or like.

The door was as solid as a rock.

3 Think of a metaphor.

The door is a dragon, guarding the exit.

4 Think of some personification.

The door begged me to enter the room.

5 Think of an onomatopoeia word for what a door does.

The door banged shut.

6 Write your answer in the table.

The door	was as solid as a rock.	(simile)
	is a dragon, guarding the exit.	(metaphor)
	begged me to enter the room.	(personification)
	banged shut.	(onomatopoeia)

Now try these questions.

1 Join the phrases and clauses to the type of figurative language they illustrate.

as high as a kite	the car screamed	the girl mumbled

| simile | metaphor | personification | onomatopoeia |

| the fog was a grey blanket | the crisps crunched | flew like a bird |

(1 mark each)

/6

2 Complete these similes:

a) as tall as ——————— b) as white as ———————

c) as wise as ——————— d) as hungry as ———————

e) as brave as ——————— f) as proud as ———————

g) as deaf as ——————— h) as blind as ———————

i) as busy as ——————— j) as slippery as ———————

(1 mark each)

/10

3 Write the onomatopoeia words for the noise made by:

a) a clock ——————— b) a plate breaking ———————

c) a bee ——————— d) a light switch ———————

e) sausages cooking ——————— f) a duck ———————

(1 mark each)

/6

4 Complete the sentence openings using the different types of figurative language shown.

The bus	(simile)
	(metaphor)
	(personification)
	(onomatopoeia)

The flowers	(simile)
	(metaphor)
	(personification)
	(onomatopoeia)

The wind	(simile)
	(metaphor)
	(personification)
	(onomatopoeia)

(1 mark each)

/12

CHALLENGE Find examples of figurative language and explain why the author used them and why they are effective.